CREDIT BOSS

A Step By Step Plan to Understanding Your Credit and How to Repair Your Credit Like The Pros

Bianca Jules

Bianca Jules

1st Edition

Copyright 2018 by Bianca Jules

All rights reserved.

This Publication is designed to provide accurate and authoritative information regarding the same subject matter covered. It is sold with the understanding that the author and publisher does not lend legal or other professional advice. If required, it is advised to seek legal and professional expert advice when necessary. No part of this book may be reproduced in any form without written consent of the publisher, excepting brief quotes used in reviews.

Printed in the United States of America

ISBN- 9781983691959

From the Author

Let's settle a few things, the reason most people remain financially broke their entire lives is not because they suffer from bad credit. Every thought, beliefs, word they have focused and words they have spoken has manifested its way to them. Bad credit is simply the result of the vibration and energy they have put out in the ether. For starters and context, I am a person who believes in the power and faith of God and the will of yourself. I believe that man has also been given the creative power of manifestation being created in the same image of God. Therefore, when I discuss wealth and the mindset that is required to attain wealth, I am talking about the power of words and thoughts that you play as a recording in your life. Most people are unaware of the power that they truly possess and that everything all around us contains energy. This is proven in the very science and mathematical equations of infinite energy that it can never be created or destroyed, and that energy is in all things. All the thoughts and words we have spoken yesterday, have undoubtedly, created the very conditions and circumstances that we experience today. Whether we have grown from childhood hearing parents, or a dominant society that repeatedly enforces fear and negative words involving money, increase, and wealth, these very words have a strong influence in shaping our current mindset and thoughts regarding the very subject of money.

Table of Contents

INTRODUCTION 7

CHAPTER 1 CREATING A MINDSET OF WEALTH 11

CHAPTER 2 WHAT IS CREDIT AND YOUR ROLE IN THE SYSTEM 15

CHAPTER 3 THE CREDIT BUREAUS AND HOW THEY REALLY OPERATE 27

CHAPTER 4 CREDIT SCORES ARE NOT CREATED EQUAL 37

CHAPTER 5 GETTING YOUR WHOLE P.I.E 49

CHAPTER 6 HOW CREDIT REPAIR REALLY WORKS 61

CHAPTER 7 HOW TO DISPUTE INACCURATE ACCOUNTS................................. 69

CHAPTER 8 ADVANCED CREDIT DISPUTING TECHNIQUES............................ 117

CHAPTER 9 DEALING WITH IDENTITY THEFT 133

CHAPTER 10 HOW TO USE PAY FOR DELETION METHOD............................... 141

CHAPTER 11 LEGAL LIABILITY AND STATUTE OF LIMITATIONS..................... 151

CHAPTER 12 BUILDING BUSINESS CREDIT PROFILES AND SCORES 159

CONCLUSION 167

ABOUT THE AUTHOR 169

Introduction

It is my hope and mission that as many people understand how credit works and its ability to help you attain wealth when used the right way. But too often, most people cringe when they hear the word "credit".

It is also my hope that those who aspire to investigate their credit and apply their understanding to know that the possibility of the power of its leverage can free them from debt. The credit system is complicated, scary, and sometimes might even appear overwhelming, but rest assured, it can be understood and even controlled if you possess the right knowledge to understand and apply the knowledge available at your disposal for reference. We should all know that knowledge unapplied serves us no good for increase

With this book in your hands, it is my hope that you become a credit master. You will know exactly what your credit scores are based on and how you can control them for your ultimate benefit. You will learn the secrets the credit bureaus often keep hidden and don't want you to know about their computers, their systems, and the unscrupulous operations of their past. You will learn about their current unethical creditor tactics that are being used to ruin your credit. You will even have access to credit bureau dispute methods, letters, and advanced letters which will all help you remove inaccurate and negative items from your credit report. You will understand overall that credit scoring and fundability of your credit profile is not merely based on your credit score, but also the metrics of your personal credit profile that you have not been taught to understand how things all work together in terms of credit scoring.

This book is designed to give you a step-by-step process of understanding, repairing and optimizing your credit. You will be able to first understand the credit system itself, then know everyone's roles in the credit system, and, finally, you will be able to overcome your credit problems once and for all. You can have excellent credit and the credit system can be beaten. But you must claim it in mindset first and have a clear mental picture of your vision of your credit. This book will show you how to navigate the understanding of it all.

"Therefore I say unto you, What things soever ye desire, when ye pray, believe that ye receive them, and ye shall have them."

Mark 11:24

Chapter 1
Creating A Mindset of Wealth

Your mindset has created your present financial atmosphere- whether you presently experience abundant or lack. However, nothing stays the same. You have the ability if put into action, the absolute power to change your financial circumstances at any given point in time.

So, with this book, I want to highlight the understanding of mindset and its purpose in your life to consciously shape your thoughts as a foundation to wealth.

Growing up, my mother and father were very influential in my life, whether directly and indirectly. When I was 7 years old, despite my childhood of poverty living in a single parent home with my mother and younger brother, I made a self-declaration that I would not live a life of poverty. I made up in my mind at that time, that I would live a life opposite of the poverty I experienced throughout childhood. From that point on, I enjoyed creating mental images in my mind of fullness, freedom, and travel. My mother always spoke words of wisdom in my life and encouraged me at 11 years old to "seek wisdom" in everything I did. It was from there those words forever stuck with me. I fervently sought through the pages of my childhood bible and from this very young age, I was guided on the path of seeking knowledge beyond my present state and knowing that all wisdom was understood with a mind of understanding. Use your mind to form a mental image of what you want and hold your vision with unwavering faith and purpose to keep your mindset on the path to attain your goals.

Your words work in agreement with your mindset. Words carry such a vibration that can be seen through the evidence of the passing of time the things you have created with it- whether positive or negative. The vibration of words carries with them something so powerful. It is important to understand the workings of these concepts to set a foundation of wealth because obtaining wealth is not about just hard work or being intelligent or the number of degrees one has obtained in this society. If this were so, how do you explain those who have reached millionaire status despite being high school and or college dropouts.

I have come to realize that there is opportunity of wealth all around because wealth is infinite because it comes from the supreme Creator. Whether you see wealth and money as a lack or in enough provision, you are right in both cases.

It is important to lay the foundation of positive and certain mindset and way of thinking in life when understanding the power of credit. Because the power of wealth and resources is unlimited, I am speaking from just one of the MANY ways to get ahead financially in this life. We all carry the power within us to create the life that we so desire. And it is also up to us individually to seek and find this Power within. When we understand this power that we all have inside of us, it is critical to ignite it and put it to use.

In terms of credit, its purpose, and how to win at the game of credit by leveraging it, has merely become one of the areas that I have become an expert in after divulging much time, thought, practice and energy into over the years by not only helping myself but to help many of my clients and others gain the understanding that by leveraging the use of their improved credit- it is as an avenue to jumpstart their ability of attaining financial success.

It is essential in life to have the right tools to build a life of financial success. It is also essential to use those tools in the right way, knowing that the foundation of the right tools include the power of mindset, the power of words, and purposeful Vision. The more you have the right foundation and application of this foundation and framework of financial success, the more you will attract the emotions and energy of the attributes you will need on your path of financial success. So, before I begin to expand on the exact processes to put into action to repair one's credit, let me say that overall you must have a positive outlook and open mind in order to put any of these instructions to work in action. If you have a negative mindset regarding anything, you will produce negative results. I encourage those readers to be aware of personal mindsets while working to achieve these tried and proven and strategies in the credit repair process.

"For as he thinketh in his heart, so *is* he:

Proverbs 23:7

Chapter 2
What is Credit and Your Role in the System

Credit is defined as an agreement between a creditor or lender and a borrower in which the consumer assumes something of value in agreement to repay the creditor, based on certain terms.

Credit is used in just about every financial area of our current society, that is nearly impossible to operate without it. Even when you apply for a job nowadays, many employers will also check your credit history to gauge you as a worthy candidate for an employed position. From car dealers, banks, credit card companies, mortgage companies, signature loan companies, pay day advances, even student loan agencies, are just a few of the many sources who extend credit to individuals.

When you apply for new credit, these creditors review your credit profile to determine your risk of repaying that debt. Based on your risk you might get approved or denied.

If you do get approved, the repayment terms will again be based on the quality of your credit profile. The better your credit profile and the higher your score, the better terms you will receive.

When your credit profile is damaged, you will be charged higher interest based on that risk. The rate of interest will vary based on many factors, but interest charges can be significant. One credit card company in 2009 even released a credit card with an 89% APR!

Importance of Credit

Your life is your credit. If you have ever been denied a loan or even a job due to your credit, then you already know the importance your credit profile has to your life.

Most of the payments you pay each month are affected by your credit quality. Home loans, rent, car payments, credit cards, installment loans, car insurance, cell phones, health and life insurance, and even monthly utilities are all based on the quality of your credit.

From the payments you pay each month, such as whether you rent or own your dream home are based solely on your credit quality. New employers are even relying on credit to help make hiring decisions. It is impossible to hide from your credit. And as more companies rely on it to gauge risk, the importance of your credit profile is ever increasing.

But credit is also very scary. Most consumers don't know how credit works or even what their credit scores really means. One thing is for sure, there is a dramatic difference in quality of life between having bad or good credit.

Life with Bad Credit

You can live with credit issues. But every year those issues will cost you tens-of-thousands of dollars, making it hard to survive and near impossible to save money for your future.

Many consumers don't have the extra money to save due to paying tens-of-thousands of dollars each year in outlandish interest charges. Many people have no idea how much their credit is really costing them. Sure, they know that bad credit causes issues with them getting approved for new credit. But, most consumers, never REALLY know how much credit affects their day to day lives.

Bad credit ruins lives. This is one of the most shocking but REAL statements you might read in a while. The difference between living life and struggling to survive is based completely on credit quality. This entire system of the economic world revolves around credit and debt. Those that understand this are those that go on to use it to their advantage and capitalize from it by using OPM- Other people's money- that is the Money that is nearly created from thin air by using good credit to use as an investment in business and capital gains. But more on this later.

Let's look at a car as a simple example. Most people today need a vehicle to get around. We require it to get to our jobs, our kids to day care, or just to get to the store. There are an estimated 250 million car owners in the U.S. alone, so chances are pretty good you are one of them or know someone who is.

Many car owners chose to finance their vehicles and pay monthly payments until the debt is paid off. Car loans are offered to consumers based on their credit history and their credit scores, like most other loans.

And based on those credit factors, risk will be determined by the auto lender and an interest rate will be established for the consumer to pay back that loan. The payments will then be established based on the loan amount, interest rate, and term of the loan.

With good credit, you will get approved for a longer term and better interest rate. With bad credit, you will pay much greater interest on a shorter term, making your payments much higher. Maybe you already knew all that. Many consumers do, but most don't know how much that extra interest and shorter terms is really costing them.

A $20,000 car loan with good credit will cost approximately $286 monthly. This is based on a 3% interest rate for 72 months. The exact same $20,000 car loan with bad credit will cost approximately $416 monthly. This is based on a 25% interest rate for 60 months.

This is the same car, but one is costing $219 more EVERY month. The person with good credit will pay $20,600 for their car. The consumer with bad credit will pay $24,200 for the same car. That's a $4,400 difference. Essentially, the same car will cost the consumer with bad credit more than the one with good credit. Essentially meaning that you must be RICH to have Bad credit! If you have poor credit, how can you afford this? You see, the credit system capitalizes on those with poor credit.

These examples are not extreme. These are based on common interest rates you will see on a $20,000 auto loan.

Rent and home expenses are another area where customers get taken for great amounts of interest.

A $100,000 mortgage costs a good credit consumer $577 monthly and $207,720 over 30 years. The same home would cost a family with challenged credit $841 monthly and $302,760 over 30 years.

The consumer with good credit will pay $264 less per month and save $95,040 over the lifetime of the loan. That means the person with bad credit will pay $95,040 more in interest for a $100,000 loan, due to their credit.

Credit cards might cost $116 more monthly based on credit. Utility payments are higher, insurance payments are more, and so are many other regular family expenses.

Most people know credit has an adverse effect on their life. But the truth is, bad credit controls their lives. Outrageous amounts of extra interest are being charged each month. That debt and those higher payments strap most families, forcing them to live paycheck-to-paycheck.

If even one emergency arises, many consumers in this position are susceptible to a total financial catastrophe. With bad credit, their lives are just like a house of cards waiting to collapse. I ask again, can you afford to live this way? This is not life, not a fullness of life at all.

Consumers with credit issues don't have high open limits to use in case of emergencies. When a transmission goes out or a child needs emergency dental treatment, pay day loans become about the only option to get money in a pinch. The rates on those are extremely high, making them almost impossible to pay off.

Life is tough with bad credit, tough. With no available credit, one emergency can wipe you out. And there is no extra money each month, due to hundreds-of-dollars each month spent on excessive interest charges.

Many then are so caught up with financial survival, they forget about how innocently it all began. Instead, they are caught in a trap, a literal never-ending cycle, which few recover from.

The Bad Credit Trap

I call this the Mouse on a Wheel- Bad Credit Trap. This is a trap most consumers will never get out of. The system won't naturally allow them to recover. The system inevitably is a whole entire trap in itself. From all the programming engrained in our thinking from the funneled pipeline from primary to grade school, on to the college funnel to a job working for an employer, we are taught financial traps. From being taught that a high school education won't allow you to make it financially or earn a decent wage job. Or being taught the latter that going into thousands of dollars of financial debt in order to earn a college degree. Many college graduates learn that not only do most jobs obtained starting salary do not pay enough to cover the amount of their student loans obtained to gain the job of their earned degree. Yet worst, some discover that in the present times, their initial college degree is not enough to earn them their desired wages, so they are told to earn more in wages, more degrees are necessary and therefore mount more of their growing pile of financial student loan debt in their quest of obtaining more degrees.

I have heard clients tell me how good their credit was before it went bad. But I have never had even one client with good credit tell me their credit was bad and it suddenly got better.

Most with bad credit never recover. That is a fact. And the reason is that the system is against them from the start. Consumers with credit issues are not in their situations because they are bad people. They are sucked into a trap that most simply don't know how to recover from.

Credit problems usually stem from an uncontrollable event. Some have a car crash or medical issue that compiles medical bills. Many others go through divorce or have credit too young, leading to issues where a default or late payment occurs.

There are thousands of reasons things happen, but let's just say life happens. And when life happens, and even one account gets paid late, a domino effect of a downward credit spiral then begins to happen. Even if the late payment was for one credit card, most other card companies will claim their risk is higher.

Several things start to happen at this point. First, many creditors will lower their limits. If a creditor lowers the high credit limit on an account, the credit score always goes down. This is due to 1/3 of your credit score being based on your Available Credit, which you will find more about in later chapters.

Now the consumer has less available credit, right when they obviously need it. Plus, with lower available credit, they will face more overdraft fees. And the credit scores drop, and risk increases for all other accounts, due to the lower score.

Now creditors will start to increase interest rates due to the increased risk. All creditors can't do this, but in the fine print, many reserves the right to do just this. The higher rates mean the payments also increase. The consumer is now faced with higher payments on several of their accounts, not to mention having to pay their original late fees.

Eventually, this leads to many consumers going late on other payments. Then things start to get bad, really fast. In a very short period, credit that once was good is now left destroyed.

This means all new credit the consumer applies for will only be approved at high risk rates. This costs hundreds more dollars every month and radically deteriorates the consumer's quality of life, for many years to come.

Most consumers continue to then struggle all their life with this cycle. The high interest rates and payments leave them living paycheck-to-paycheck. And they commonly go late on their payments after that, as they struggle to pay outrageous high interest rates and payments.

This is the Bad Credit Cycle. Many times, it starts with one unavoidable late payment. But in the end, it costs most any chance of having a healthy financial future.

Life with Good Credit

Now, oppositely, life with good credit is an entirely different story. Many people believe they want to be rich, financially. But what many don't realize is that their fantasy life has less to do with being rich and more to do with having good credit.

Mercedes Benz is a great symbol of car luxury. Many dream of having the opportunity to own one. In their dreams, they fantasize about being rich or driving a Mercedes. With good credit, a brand new Mercedes Benz can cost about $320 a month. Even a luxury home can be financed for less than $1,000 monthly at low market interest rates.

The secret to wealth, in many cases, has less to do with being rich and more to do with credit quality. Even a crazy dream like walking into a store and buying whatever you want or buying a car on your credit can be reached if you have good credit, and even if you are not wealthy.

Good credit won't stand in the way of getting a good job or getting approved for a new credit card at 0% interest rates. Good credit makes living the dream of home ownership a reality.

Credit lines are issued to consumers based on their credit quality. With good credit, it is common for consumers to receive credit lines and credit cards for $10,000 or higher. In many cases the interest on those cards is also less than 3%, making them ideal for many situations, especially emergencies. Good credit creates peace of mind for this reason.

Let me tell you a little lender secret here. Good credit clients in most businesses are treated better than those with credit issues. Auto dealers, banks, mortgage companies may try not to, but most do treat good credit customers superior.

I don't agree with this at all, but I saw it every day once I became the owner of great credit. My personal scores were from the scores around the low 600's to scores over 780 and 800. Trust me when I say that good credit customers are offered better deals than those with credit issues.

The main reason is that good credit buyers are stereotyped as smart, intellectual, educated, people who do their research and will leave in a minute if they think they are being taken advantage of. So, this fear has most sales managers coddling good credit prospects.

Today, good credit is like being rich. When you have it you are treated better, can spend more and pay less, and absolutely afford to have the life of your dreams.

Good credit is king in this capitalist structure and the hidden secret in this society. And this secret of the credit system, secrets behind your credit scores, and even a proven secret system to correct your credit will be revealed in the following chapters.

Your Role in the Credit System

As important as your credit is, most people believe that there is someone looking out for them and that the credit bureaus job is to make sure that their personal credit reporting is accurate and reflecting a clear picture of their history and personal identity. Well let me assure you that this idea of thinking couldn't be further than the truth. This is the common belief I have always heard from clients. They believe that surely the government, the bureaus, or even the creditors are insuring that reported data is accurate and correct.

But the sad truth is, nobody is watching out for you at all. You are the ONLY person involved with your credit who benefits from your credit profile being both positive and accurate.

The credit bureaus, like many companies, do have to abide by certain federal and state laws. They are also required to investigate credit disputes based on certain criteria per laws like the Fair Credit Reporting Act. But the credit bureaus don't question what creditors report, unless they themselves are questioned on it. You see, you are not an actual customer of the credit bureaus, nor are you the main concern of their reporting. You are actually the PRODUCT and your information is for sale. The actual customers of the credit bureaus are the corporations and creditors who do the reporting and provide the credit bureaus with your data. You see, your credit is not personal and you a simply a data point to the credit bureaus to which they report on. In later chapters, I will demonstrate how to use this fact to your advantage in repairing your credit.

Creditors also must abide by state and federal laws. But most reporting creditors don't have divisions within their companies where they validate what they are reporting. The credit bureaus and creditors do have one thing in common in regard to the reporting of your data. They both make more money the worse your credit is.

To investigate this more, let's look at the roles everyone plays in the credit reporting process.

Chapter 3
The Credit Bureaus and How they REALLY Operate

The Fait Credit Reporting Act refers to the credit bureaus as Consumer Reporting Agencies or CRAs. The "Big 3" credit bureaus are Trans Union, Equifax, and Experian. There is a fourth reporting CRA known as Innovis, which creditors rarely use.

These are private *for-profit* companies who make money by collecting and selling consumer information. Let's look at the history of each of these four Consumer Reporting Agencies.

Trans Union

Trans Union got its start back in 1968 as a holding company created by Union Tank Car Company. The following year, in 1969, Trans Union purchased Credit Bureau of Cook County (CBCC), entering into the credit business.

In subsequent years, TU continued to purchase major cities' credit bureaus and exclusive rights with many of their creditors. Their vision was to create a national credit database from what then was not more than simple file cards. TU obtained over 3.5 million of those file cards with their purchase of CBCC alone and continued to combine millions more to create the database they have today.

Trans Union continued to grow and expand their business, most recently purchasing True Credit in 2002. This was their first attempt to sell to consumers directly and has been an ever-increasing aspect of their business ever since.

Today Trans Union is based out of Chicago, Illinois, and operates over 249 offices nationwide and offices in 25 countries on 5 continents.

Equifax

Equifax is the oldest and largest credit bureau in existence today. They were originally founded in 1898, 70 years before the creation of Trans Union.

Two brothers, Cator and Guy Woolford, created the company. Cator got the idea from his grocery business, where they collected customers' names and evidence of credit worthiness. He then sold that list to other merchants to offset his own business costs.

The success led Cator and his attorney brother, Guy, to Atlanta to start what would become one of the most powerful industries in existence today.

Retail Credit Company was born, and local grocers started using the Woolford service, which expanded rapidly. By the early 1900s the service had expanded from grocers to the insurance industry.

Retail Credit Company continued to grow into one of the largest credit bureaus by the 1960s, with nearly 300 branches in operation. They collected all kinds of consumer data, even rumors about people's marital lives and childhood. They were also scrutinized for selling this data to just about anyone who would buy it.

In the late '60s, Equifax started to compile their data onto computers, giving many more companies access to purchase this data. They also continued to purchase many more of their smaller competitors, becoming larger and attracting the attention of our Federal government.

In response, the US Congress met in 1971, and enacted the Fair Credit Reporting Act. This new law was the first to govern the information credit bureaus and regulate what they were allowed to collect and sell. Equifax was charged with violating this law a few years later and even more government restrictions were implemented.

Equifax was no longer allowed to misrepresent themselves when conducting consumer investigations and employees were not given bonuses anymore based on the negative information they were collecting, which was standard practice in the past.

It is alleged that due to the tarnished reputation all this left on Retail Credit Company, they changed their name to Equifax (Equitable Factual Information) shortly after in 1979.

Throughout the 1980s, Equifax along with Experian and Trans Union, split up the rest of the smaller credit rating agencies amongst them, adding 104 of those to Equifax's portfolio. They then continued to grow, taking aligning with CSC Credit Services and another 65 additional bureaus.

Equifax has continued to grow, now maintaining over 401 million consumer credit records worldwide. They also expanded their services to direct consumer credit monitoring in 1999. Today Equifax is based out of Atlanta, Georgia, and has employees in 14 countries.

Experian

Experian was formerly a division of TRW, an automotive electronics giant. TRW was originally founded in 1901 as the Cleveland Cap Screw Company. They started producing screws and bolts and grew to produce many parts for the aviation and automobile industry.

In the early 1960s, TRW started a consumer credit information bureau, collecting and selling consumer data, and eventually became known as TRW Information Systems. TRW Information Systems continued compiling data and were the first to start offering consumers direct credit report access in 1986.

In 1991, rampant problems started appearing with TRW reported credit data. Thousands of people in a town in Vermont had tax liens inaccurately reporting against them. Similar cases started appearing in the entire northeast, forcing the deletion of countless tax liens across the states of Vermont, Rhode Island, New Hampshire, and Maine

Dozens of law suits were filed against TRW, claiming sloppy procedures to create credit files, lack of response to consumer complaints, and re-reporting previously deleted incorrect data. All cases were settled out of court.

Then TRW created a database known as the Constituent Relations Information Systems (CRIS). This system's sole purpose was to gather personal data on 8,000 politicians who had an opinion of TRW.

In 1996, TRW was purchased for over 1 billion dollars by a private group of investors, and then acquired by CCN, the largest credit reporting company in the United Kingdom. Their name was also changed to Experian.

Today, Experian offers their services in over 65 countries, employing over 15,000 people and has their main headquarters in Dublin, Ireland. Their stock is sold on the London Stock Exchange.

Innovis

Innovis once was ACB Services and was founded in 1970. Innovis is not used by many creditors, at all. Verizon is one of the main creditors who still do use Innovis. But Innovis is said to be the first CRA to use databases and automation to capture and store consumer data.

Fannie Mae and Freddie Mac, as of 2001, started requiring that mortgage companies also report to Innovis, which was a huge step for their future. Innovis offers two main services including a list of people who have recently changed addresses and another list of consumers who have a challenged credit history.

Since 1898, when Equifax began, companies have been collecting and selling consumer data. Today the three major credit bureaus all house hundreds-of-millions of profiles for individual consumers.

How this data is valued is another interesting and revealing point to discuss.

Lexis Nexis

Another major data furnisher of public records is Lexis Nexis. Your public records are supplied by this 3rd party supplier and record keeper. Lexis Nexis directly supplies additional public record data collected to the 3 major credit bureaus. Your public records contain many of the derogatory items such as tax liens, foreclosures, bankruptcies, public judgements, etc.

Why the Credit Bureaus Love Bad Credit

Your credit profile is made up of data collected by creditors, then reported to the credit bureaus. The bureaus then make a profit by selling this data in reports, leads, and other methods to creditors for the purpose of issuing new credit or soliciting you for credit.

For example, when a creditor, such as CHASE, wants to offer you new credit, they purchase a data list from the credit bureaus. This list might be of consumers with credit scores from 550-620, for example. The bureaus then profit my selling that list to CHASE and CHASE will then use that list to send mailers to you soliciting you to apply for their credit card.

In the data selling world, credit challenged consumers with sub-prime credit are always more valuable. This means a creditor will pay more for a list of consumers who are 30 days late on their mortgage than a consumer with a perfect pay history.

This is simply due to supply and demand. Very few companies want the perfect pay history consumers, so this data has a low value. But there is a significant amount of sub-prime companies who will pay top dollar for this data.

Sub-prime credit card companies, auto and home loan, credit repair, loan modification, short sale companies, and even debt consolidation are just a few company types who pay big money for these types of leads.

Companies also pay more for "triggers" or "selects" for consumer leads. This means they pay more for bankruptcy leads, high credit card balances, late payments on credit cards, COLLECTIONS, 30-90-day late payments, foreclosures, and even late payments on mortgages.

CHASE won't pay much for a list of good credit customers. In comparison, a bankruptcy company will pay a lot more for a list of consumers who filed bankruptcy within the last 30 days. That list is much more specific and would cost about TWICE as much from the bureaus.

So, the credit bureaus actually make MORE money the worse your credit is. This is NOT an opinion, but a clear FACT. It is NOT in the credit bureaus' best interest to help ensure your credit report is accurate. Actually, they make more money if your credit is bad.

The only reason they allow you to dispute accounts on your report is that they are obligated by law to do so. These laws were created due to the rampant credit bureau abuse and mishandling of consumer data.

The credit bureaus are not your friends and they do not benefit by you having a positive credit profile. So, don't expect them to be looking out for the accuracy of your credit profile. This is why it is imperative that you learn to correct your own personal data.

Your Creditors/ Data Furnishers

Creditors in the credit equation are known as Data Furnishers. They are the agencies who offer financing to consumers, then report the pay histories back to the credit reporting agencies or the credit bureaus.

Some other personal information is also given by creditors, including consumers' names, date of birth, social security number, address, prior addresses, current employer, previous employer, and even inquiries for credit applications used to determine spending patterns. Everything they can collect from the consumer and report back to the bureaus by law, they do collect and report.

Most data furnishers are private and public for-profit companies. They make money based on lending to consumers and earning a return through interest. This interest is based on risk. The higher your risk, the more you pay in interest. And in most cases, your interest rate is tied directly to your credit scores. The lower your scores, the higher your interest rate will be.

Credit card companies don't make anything on 0% cards. But the minute you go late on your payment, your interest rate skyrockets. This is where they make their money, on 13% and higher interest rate charges.

A published study shows that some companies make 3 times more money on their sub-prime clients as they do their prime clients. The worse your credit is, the more your creditors charge, and the more profits they make on you.

This is why your creditors monitor your credit report frequently. Any decrease to your score or adverse information on your report can then be used to raise your interest rates, even if you didn't go late on that creditor's account.

But notice, you have probably never had a creditor monitor your credit then politely inform you of misreported information on your report. This is because the worse your credit is, the more money your creditors will make. And you will find that credit errors are rarely in your favor, for the same reason.

BOTH your creditors and the credit bureaus make more money the worse your credit is. It is in their benefit that your credit is bad, so don't expect them to spend a lot of time ensuring that your credit profile is accurate and positive.

Your Role

Every time you apply for new credit data is collected from you. The data is collected and then submitted to the credit bureau as an inquiry.

The inquiry comes back to the creditor as a credit file. Your credit file consists of information on your prior credit accounts, your credit score, and your residence and employment information.

This information is then used by the creditor to offer or deny you financing. In most cases, the creditor won't even let you have a copy of the report they are using. You have to order your own, making it even harder to ensure the data they are seeing is accurate.

But due to prior credit bureau abuse and misreporting of information, you are entitled to one free copy of your credit report each year. This is because the federal government is not monitoring your report for accuracy, but instead, they are depending on you to self-regulate your own credit profile.

You are expected to get a copy of your report each year to make sure it is accurate. When you do this, you will always want to check all the data very carefully on your report for accuracy. YOU are the ONLY person dealing with your credit who benefits by having an accurate and positive credit.

So, take it upon yourself to get a copy of your free report, dispute any inaccurate information, and manage your credit wisely. You are the only one who benefits when your profile is positive and accurate, the power is held in your hands to get it corrected.

Chapter 4
Credit Scores are not Created Equal

You are probably familiar with your credit score. Nowadays you can gain access to your credit reports and your credit scores much easier than in the past. This is because government regulations are now giving consumers more access to this once highly secretive credit system.

Knowing your credit score is important but knowing how your credit score works is essential. Once you know and understand the components of your credit score and how they work, you will then be able to make small adjustments and make significant increases to your scores.

The first thing to know is that there are many different credit scores in existence. Each of these is based on a separate credit scoring model.

The Different Credit Score Models

There are hundreds of different credit scoring models. Most of the commonly used models come from a company named Fair Isaac, which is commonly termed FICO score. FICO does statistical calculations of risk and summarizes it in a numerical value, which is your credit score. Your credit score is all about collection of data algorithms that are used to predict your financial behaviors.

Fair Isaac creates scoring models which gauge a consumer's risk in paying back a debt. To be more specific, their calculations are designed to gauge a consumer's risk of going *90 days late on an account in the next 2 years*. The greater your risk of going 90 days late, the lower your credit score will be.

Fair Isaac then sells their scoring models to the credit bureaus Trans Union, Equifax, and Experian. They also sell hundreds of other specialized scoring models to other industries. There are Mortgage Industry and Auto Industry Option scoring models, credit card models, banking industry models, global models, and hundreds more. Under the FICO score you can have many scores for each industry which are used by that industry in terms of lending.

Many industries want their own specific models. This is why if you apply for a car loan or mortgage, they will always pull different credit scores than you will pull on your own.

For example, the Auto Industry Option scoring model rates six specific auto history accounts types heavier than all other accounts. If a consumer has a repossession, their Auto Industry score pulled by a car dealer will be less than if the consumer pulled their own consumer score.

The auto lenders care more about your past auto history more than anything else. So, when they pull their score, any bad or good auto history will have a greater impact on your scores than on any consumer report you may pull. These variables are known by Fair Isaac as "scorecards".

Credit card models will rate credit card late payments heavier than other models will. Each industry specific model will be impacted more if accounts are paid late or defaulted on within that specific industry.

There are also general models like *Classic FICO* and *FICO 08* and the recently introduced FICO 09, which are the models you can go online and pull your own score for.

FICO vs. FAKE-O Scores

Various versions of credit scoring have been attempted by financial institutions for over the last 60 years. FICO became the industry leader in consumer credit scoring in the late 1990's. Fair Isaac is NOT a credit bureau, in fact, it is a completely separate company that sells scoring software to lenders. This software scores the data that lenders download from the credit bureaus when pulling a credit report and used with over 90% of lenders. The three-digit number that results from this software analysis is called the FICO® Credit Score that ranges from 350-850.

Industry specific credit score wholesalers will provide mortgage brokers and mortgage lenders with mortgage-specific credit reports, to which mortgage lenders can subscribe and purchase. An example of how the delivery of credit reports and scores to your mortgage broker is a two-step process detailed below:

1. A mortgage broker typically enters your information into the credit report provider's software on their computer.

2. The wholesaler's software pulls your credit profile data from the three national credit bureaus and applies the mortgage-specific FICO score software to your credit profile data and then delivers a mortgage credit report and the accompanying mortgage scores. These credit scores are legitimate credit scores—FICO® mortgage scores.

The mortgage-specific FICO® software evaluates your credit history with your past mortgages. The score that is printed out on your mortgage credit report reflects this exact screening process. Currently FICO® Scoring software has over 88 products to help financial institutions grade borrower trustworthiness according to purchase type.

By using industry-specific screening software, lenders lessen the risk of financial loss. FICO® scoring software have been developed for mortgage companies, auto dealers, credit card companies, health care insurers, telecom companies, and cellphone providers, among many others.

What are FAKE-O Scores?

Until recently, credit scoring was a well-kept secret. Many people were surprised when they found out they were being financially judged by a number that they not only didn't understand but had no control over.

As public awareness increased, the media started making a fuss about this "secret" FICO score that could be used to make or break a lending decision. To remedy this situation, Congress ordered the credit bureaus to offer free credit reports once per year so consumers could monitor and take control of the information in their credit profile. Of course, that didn't actually solve the problem—some actually believe this made things worse.

Consumers didn't just want copies of their credit reports—they wanted access to their credit scores. Since the credit bureaus now had to offer credit reports by mandate imposed by Congress, the credit bureaus began offering credit reports via the internet (up to this point, consumers had to receive their credit reports through mail). And since the credit bureaus are all about profit, the credit bureaus began to provide the Congress-mandated credit *reports* for free while charging a fee for the actual credit *score*. Unfortunately, the credit scores that they offered were completely useless.

Today, over 90% all lenders use some version of the FICO® scoring software. But the credit scores that the bureaus began to sell to consumers on the internet were not the scores lenders used. Any credit score that does not have the FICO® registered trademark is commonly termed as a FAKE-O score. TrueCredit.com, FreeCreditReport.com, CreditReport.com, CreditKarma.com, Vantage score, and most other credit report monitoring services offered on the internet are FAKE-O scores and cannot be accurately used to evaluate what lenders will see when they pull your credit report.

Your actual FICO scores can be retrieved from score websites directly from FICO at myFICO.com. As the name suggests, the scores that are offered by this site are actual FICO® scores—28 of them. The beauty of the myFICO.com credit report is that it offers the same industry scores offered by car dealers, mortgage companies, and credit card companies, etc.

The Credit Score Breakdown

The FICO software has over 85 software versions that measure predictive analytics. The scores that are consumer scores viewed from myfico.com are actually unweighted scores, meaning that these scores hold little to no value. The scores that hold the most value are those industry specific scores that are gauged by your specific financial behavior for that industry as previously mentioned. Those industry specific scores are specific to the mortgage, auto, credit card and banking industries and so forth.

FICO also measures over 40 points of data; however they only publish to the general public 5 of the main factors. Of the 40 factors that FICO scores, did you know that only 10 are associated with negative factors? Yes, that means that you have about 30 OTHER scoring opportunities to increase your score regardless of currently reporting negative accounts. The 5 main scoring factors are built on the following ingredients:

Payment History-   35%

Your payment history is the largest aspect of your credit score, as you might expect. In total, your pay history accounts for **35%** of your total score.

This aspect of your total score calculation is based on your prior payment history with your creditors. Late payments, defaulted accounts, bankruptcies, and all other negative information on your credit report have the greatest effect.

The more recent the late payment, the greater the damage is to your credit score. If you go late on your mortgage this month, the Mortgage Industry Option scoring model could drop your scores over 120 points. That is with only one 30-day late payment!

The scoring model is based on your potential to go 90 days late on an account within the next 2 years. Any recent late payments are a big reflection that you will default, and your credit score plummets as a result.

Your creditor cannot report you late unless you are 30 days late. But they will claim they need 10 days to process your payment. So, don't think just because you mailed your payment on the 25th day that they will not report you late.

All together, your entire history of payment counts for 35% of your total scores. The more positive accounts you have and the less negative means a much higher credit score.

Percentage of High-Credit Used-   30%

The second largest factor in your credit scores is the amount you owe in relation to your high credit limits.

If you are carrying high credit card balances, you can hurt your credit scores almost as much as paying the account late every month. This is because if you go late you affect 35% of your score, but if you use a high percentage of your available credit you affect 30% of your scores.

This is why I recommend getting approved for new credit. Obtaining a large limit account, such as a $5,000 line-of-credit which requires no credit check. This high balance account will really open up the available credit on the report and increase the scores.

This aspect of your credit score has several different factors. The first factor is your relation of balances you owe on all of your accounts in relation to the high credit limits on those accounts. Once again, this takes into consideration balances on all of your accounts combined. Your credit score also takes into account balances in relation to high credit limits on your individual accounts.

For example, you will be scored higher if you owe 30% or less on your credit card accounts. This means if you have a high credit limit of $1,000, you will have a higher score if you maintain a balance of $300 or less.

For revolving accounts, such as credit cards, you want to keep the smallest balances while still keeping a balance. Don't pay the account to 0, and not use it. If you stop using the account, your credit score is not increasing. Pay it as close to 1% as you can, but make sure you keep your balances below 30%.

Your scores will also be lower due to higher balances on installment loans, car loans, mortgages, and other non-revolving accounts. This is why your credit scores will always be immediately lower if you open any of these accounts new. A new car loan, for example, will lower your scores once it goes on your report. How much lower depends on your spread of other accounts.

As your loans and mortgages are paid down over time, your scores will steadily increase. This is why one of the best things you can do for your credit is open accounts and pay them as agreed. Don't pay those accounts to 0 too quick, as you won't be getting credit for that account if you have no balance and no payments due.

Your score will be affected by now many open accounts have balances, how much of your total credit lines are being used, and how much of a balance you have on installment loans, such as car loans. You can directly improve your credit scores by maintaining lower balances on your accounts or spreading balances over several different accounts. You can also get approved for new high-limit accounts to increase your scores.

Length of Credit History-   15%

Your "time in the bureau" accounts for 15% of your credit score. The older you are and the longer you have had credit accounts for, the higher the score. This is why it is near impossible to get to an 800 score at a young age. As you have more accounts throughout your life and your history grows over time, your scores will naturally increase due to this factor.

Being added as an authorized user to an account with a long pay history is another pay to increase your scores. Be careful how you do this. The new scoring models won't give you credit for most authorized user accounts unless they are family members of yours.

If you do have a family member who has had positive open accounts open for some time, see if they will add you as an authorized user on one of their accounts. They have no risk, as you won't be able to use the account unless they physically give you a card. But you will get credit on your reports, and this will increase your credit scores.

Accumulation of New Debt-   10%

Accumulation of new debt accounts for 10% of your total credit score. This aspect of your credit score is comprised of how much new debt you are applying for. It takes into consideration how many accounts you currently have open, how long it has been since you opened a new account, and how many requests you have for new credit within a 12-month time period.

If you go out today and apply for credit, that creditor requests information from the credit bureaus. This counts as an inquiry on your report. If you have a lot of inquiries in a short period of time, your scores will be impacted.

If you apply for a mortgage today, your scores might drop one point. But, if you apply for a car, a mortgage, and a few credit cards this week, your scores could drop significantly. The same applies if you have twelve car dealers pull your credit, or if one dealer has twelve banks pull your credit. A lot of credit pulls in a short period of time will have a great impact on your scores.

Don't apply for too much new credit in a short period. And don't let a lot of different creditors pull your report while applying for big purchases. You should also monitor your credit report for inquiries and dispute any that you are not familiar with or feel should be removed.

Healthy Mix of Credit Accounts- 10%

Your credit scores take into account the "mix" of credit items you have on your report. This part of your credit score is affected by what kinds of accounts you have and how many of each. The bureaus will score you higher if you have an open mortgage, 3 credit cards, 1 auto loan, and a small amount of other open accounts.

If you have a ton of credit cards, your scores will be lowered. If you have several mortgages, your scores will be lower. Any "unhealthy" account mixes lower your scores. The preferred number of credit cards is three. This means you will actually have a higher credit score if you have three open credit cards than if you have more or less than three open.

Don't run out and cancel your cards just yet. Remember, 30% of your score is comprised of your balances in relation to your high credit limit. So keep your cards open but focus on having three large balance cards for maximum impact. Maintain a healthy mix of accounts and this aspect of your credit score will be golden.

There are many different credit scoring models available for creditors. But the underlying makeup of the score is consistent. Now you know exactly how your credit score works. With this information, you can make even minor adjustments to how you use credit and see a major increase to your scores.

Chapter 5
Getting Your Whole P.I.E

I want to discuss the idea of getting your P.I.E in this system of credit. P.I.E stands for Personal Identity is Everything. Your personal identity the center of your credit profile and is more important than score when it comes to ultimately getting financed. So, in this section I want to outline the specifics of personal identity in your credit file and how your name, address, SS# is linked to your accounts.

First you will need to obtain a copy of your credit report. There is only one true way to get a free copy of your credit report with no strings attached. You can only request your report online at www.annualcreditreport.com. You can also download the request form at www.ftc.gov/credit and mail it to Credit Report Request Service, P.O. Box 105281, Atlanta, GA 30348-5281.

Or you can call toll-free to receive your credit report at 1-877-322-8228. You should be able to download your credit report immediately on the Annual Credit Report website. It will take up to 15 days to receive your report if ordering by mail or phone.

You can also sign up for a credit monitoring service and receive a free report for 30 days. But you will be required with most to give your credit card information, then auto charged after that indefinitely, until you cancel.

Every credit report will still update every 30 days, giving you constant access to your reports. This is great for constantly monitoring your credit for updates, changes, and errors.

The one I advocate for credit monitoring to keep track of your actual FICO scores is myfico.com. You can sign up for the quarterly monitoring for reports but you will have daily access with any changes and real time updates to your various FICO scores.

There are many Free monitoring sites available however, that will at least serve the purpose of monitoring your actual accounts. I do not recommend these services to keep track of your actual credit scores as they are considered FAKE-O scores. Some of the most popular sites are www.FreeCreditReport.com, www.TrueCredit.com, www.Creditkarma.com and many others found on the internet today.

Many of the bureau monitoring services use a rarely used score model. I speak of not using any of the other free scoring models or credit monitoring outside of www.myfico.com is because all the others mainly use scoring model called Vantage Score. They did this because they are owned by Trans Union and the Advantage Score is the model that the credit bureaus designed and sell. The problem is, nobody else uses that model. Car dealers, mortgage companies, and just about everyone else use a Fair Isaac model of some sort.

You probably don't want to monitor your credit progress with a scoring model that no lender uses. So, I would not use any monitoring outside of myfico.com, nor a monitoring service owned by the credit bureaus and you should be very happy with the reports you receive. You will get daily updates of your FICO scores using the mobile app and you can signup for the quarterly monitoring which should generate the quarterly reports. Outside of this, you should be able to use some of the various free monitoring like creditkarma.com to monitor the actual accounts reporting and track your dispute process. These reports are nice to have, but only essential for any kind of credit repair you might do.

If repairing your credit, you will be able to easily compare your reports month-to-month with these monitoring services. You will be able to see what was on the reports and then see the items deleted or updated on the newer reports. You can then plan out your next round of disputes, so you can see more improvement in the next 30 days.

So, try to do everything you can do to sign up for a monitoring service to keep a good eye on your credit. If you don't find a need to constantly monitor your reports, at least obtain the free copy you are entitled to each year from www.annualcreditreport.com.

How to Receive and Read Your Report

Once you have a copy of your credit report, the next step is reading and interpreting all the data on your report. The more you know the better you can monitor your reports for errors, so you can dispute any inaccurate information.

After you sign up for a credit monitoring service, sit down with your credit report. Go through your report section by section and highlight all the negative items you want to address in your disputes.

Personal Identification Profile

Every credit report has a personal profile section. It is imperative to know that the personal profile section is very important of the credit report. Personal profile is the center of the entire credit profile and the objective here is to have this area as correct and direct reporting that represents your personal identity clear and correct. Clear and accurate information will eliminate any ambiguity of your identity in terms of the FICO scoring. The personal profile area covers your current and past addresses and employers, your date of birth, and AKA information. You will first want to start by looking at the spelling of your name and your other aliases. You personal name should report as First name, Middle Initial, and Last Name. You will want to dispute any aliases you don't want on your credit report. This is one of the first areas on your report that you will need to dispute if you have multiple names and address. You will be able to increase your FICO scores up to 25+ increase by removing all multiple listings of alias names, addresses, SS#'s, employers, and phone numbers. The optimal personal identity section should report only 1 name (first, middle initial, last name), 1 address, 1 SSN, 1 telephone number and 1 employer.

In many cases, these aliases are the result of people pulling your credit report and misspelling your name. You might apply for a car loan and when they initially pull your credit, they might be a letter off when they enter your name. The credit bureaus link the pull to you, based on the social security number, and an AKA or alias appears on your credit report. So, dispute any of those multiple aliases.

Obtaining New Personal Address Profile

Addresses are linked to accounts on your credit report. If the current address you are using is linked to any bad accounts, you will need to obtain a new clean address reporting that is unassociated with any negative accounts on your report. You will be able to obtain a new address by renting a UPS post office box that will report as a street address or you can easily obtain one from ipostal.com. You can also use the address of a friend or relative's address if it is different than yours, but this must not be an address you have previously used before.

TIP: When obtaining a new address, it is advised to use a zip code address that is located in higher income neighborhoods for maximum FICO scoring points. Although lending institutions will not admit to this, many continue to use a practice called redlining.

Also to note, for all positive account that are associated with an inaccurate alias, you will want to make sure to get it updated with your current address and name. The correct address you will want to use is the accurate standard format of your address used by the USPS. You can find this by going online to USPS.com.

You will need to contact the current creditor of all positive accounts currently reporting and verify with them at least 3 times that they have the correct reporting address as the standard format. Once the creditor is reporting the corrected address, you will need to dispute all inaccurate aliases. This will also allow you to dispute any derogatory creditors that are reporting with inaccurate alias and addresses that do not align with your new address in your latter dispute letters as a basis of dispute also.

Next, you will need to update this new address on your driver's license. You can have a bank statement updated with your new address you have just obtained and have your address updated to get an updated copy of your driver's license. You will want to do this because of how the credit bureaus databases utilize a matching system. When you go to dispute any negative and derogatory accounts, your new reporting personal identity information will not link with the derogatory accounts making it easier to dispute the removal of those derogatory accounts. If there are previous addresses you don't want listed on your report, addresses you are not familiar with, misspelled addresses, or even relative's addresses, you will probably want to dispute those items to have them removed. Follow the same process with your employment information.

Dispute any inaccurate and unwanted information that appears on your report. Ensure that your name is spelled correctly, your date of birth is correct, and that your social security number is listed accurately.

Take your time and really review this section of your report. This will help reduce identity theft and ensure your credit doesn't get mixed up with others, which commonly happens.

Inquiries

An inquiry is left on your credit report when you apply for new credit. The creditor requests a credit report from the credit bureaus and an inquiry from that creditor then shows on your report. There are a few concerns you should have about inquiries. They do reveal spending patterns for you. And there are lenders who look at this while making lending decisions.

If you show a lot of inquires for credit cards in a short period, a lender offering a car loan might see you as a higher risk. Or the car dealership might even look at your inquiries to see where else you have been shopping or to see if you have been previously denied.

Employers even look at your inquiries to see what patterns might stick out. In a tough employment market, you don't want your future employer reviewing your spending habits before hiring you.

The amount of new credit you apply for accounts for 10% of your total credit score. This aspect of your credit score is based on the inquiries on your report. If you have a lot of inquires in a short period of time, your credit scores will decrease.

If you go out next week and apply for a Capital One credit card, your credit scores might decrease one point on an 850-point scale. But if you apply for seven credit cards next week, your scores might drop twenty points, due to applying for too much.

Inquiries can lower your credit scores. This is just one more reason you might want to dispute your inquiries and have them deleted. Creditors rarely respond to inquiry disputes, so this section of your credit report is easier to clean up.

Summary Section

Each credit report has an account summary section that outlines your entire report. This section shows lots of details including how many accounts you have open, closed, revolving, installment, real estate, debt outstanding, debt in collections, and more.

Take a look at each section. Do the balances owed on accounts look correct? Look at the closed and current accounts. Do those numbers look accurate? In this section you will also want to compare the different credit bureaus' information. Here you will typically see many differences. Investigate those differences as you review your report.

Don't be surprised to see big differences in what the credit bureaus report. The total amount of open and closed accounts, debt you owe, even balances and payments on individual accounts, are always reported inaccurately.

Pay close attention to the Derogatory section of the summary. Look at inquiries, public records, collection accounts, current and prior delinquencies. This is also a good section to also monitor your overall credit progress if you are disputing any inaccurate information.

Account History

Many reports break down your account history into account types. One section might be dedicated to real estate accounts, then revolving accounts, installment loans, public records, and any other categories for other account types.

Look through each section at the details on each account. You will find the creditor's name, account number, date opened, monthly payment, high balance, past due amount, and balance owed for each account.

Each account shows an Account Status, also. This might show as a number from 1-9. It also might report as a status like open, closed, or unpaid collection. The account type reflects what kind of credit account it is. Some tags are Installment, Mortgage, or Revolving.

Many times, creditors manipulate this data, also. Some account types have a greater impact on your credit score, so ensure yours are listed accurately. You can also review your Payment Status for more details on the account. This will show if it is being reported as a collection, 30 days late, or even paid as agreed.

The 24 month payment history reflects your payments for the most recent 2 years. Many monitoring service color code this section, making it easy to spot your derogatory credit items. Look for 30, 60, 90, and 120 late payments. You will also want to look for collections or accounts reported as CO. Those are all damaging to your reports and items you will want to dispute if inaccurate.

Public Records

Public records are all bankruptcies, judgments, tax liens, and all other public record types. This is one of the most harmful sections of your report and one that will demand your immediate attention. Review this section thoroughly. You will find the record type, court docket or account numbers, date filed or originally reported, and other important data that might be erroneous and need your attention.

Rarely, will you find that bankruptcies report accurately. But the bankruptcy and the accounts in the bankruptcy will remain on your credit for ten years instead of seven years like normal accounts. Judgments can remain on your credit for ten years or more. And tax liens can stay on your credit, indefinitely. This does not mean these accounts cannot be disputed and be removed from your profile. So, you will want to pay very special attention to your public records section.

TIPS FOR PUBLIC RECORDS REMOVAL

Public records disputing can be a special method in strategy. I have a particular method, but indeed there are several ways to skin a cat. One such method that I find that gets good results is always first opting out of 2nd and 3rd party credit bureaus. Then requesting your Full File Disclosure of your Lexis Nexis report. After receiving your full report, you will want to suppress this file reporting. Please note, that suppression request is separate from a freeze.

Before disputing the Bankruptcy directly, you will want to confirm all associated negative accounts that were included in the bankruptcy are previously disputed and removed. Once the associated Bankruptcy accounts are removed you are free to dispute the Bankruptcy record directly. Prepare and send a Notarized Affidavit of Fact to the Court Clerk Office or Public Records Office requesting their confirmation of your specific file to the credit bureaus. You will want to include in your letter a forwarded self addressed stamp envelope for receiving your confirmation response back from the courts. This letter will be in your favor as courts do NOT report directly to confirm any records with the credit bureaus. The credit bureau agencies search a public PACER system to search for court documents. https://www.pacer.gov/

A further tip about the credit bureaus is that they only have access to your last 4 digits of your SSN with regards to bankruptcy records. So knowing this fact they use PACER system as a matching system without having your full SSN. Therefore it is not uncommon for inaccurate information regarding a public record to be placed and reported on your account. True verification of public records are only done by physical request in person at the physical court location where the record was filed. After 2 years from discharge, the records have to be requested physically from storage. Therefore, no credit bureau is actually verifying ANY public record according to FRCA.

With the confirmation letter you have received from the courts confirming that they do not report to the credit bureaus, you will attach that letter to another notarized AFFIDAVIT confirming to the bureaus of your contact to the courts directly that they have NOT verified the public record with the courts as they previously claimed and that the courts confirmed that they do not report or verify any public record with the bureaus. This will be a smoking gun to have the record removed and DEMAND FOR DELETION. Be sure to make copies of ALL your mailed letter copies as this will also be substantiated evidence should you need to file a small claims case against the bureau if otherwise.

All the other details

Each credit monitoring service has its own special sections of information they give you on your credit reports. Some of these are details on factors affecting your credit scores, detailed overviews of credit patters, and details on more discrepancy items on your reports.

Take the time to review these sections. There is an abundance of information that you are paying for with the service.

So, enjoy the bonuses. If you have not recently obtained a copy of your credit report, stop reading this book and please do so now. It is essential that you know what is on your report. This is the first step to insuring you have a positive credit and financial future.

Chapter 6
How Credit Repair Really Works

Credit repair is the systematic disputing of erroneous, inaccurate, and unverifiable credit report accounts for the purpose of having them deleted.

The Fair Credit Reporting Act originally became law in 1971. This law allows consumers many rights, including the right to dispute inaccurate information on their credit report.
This law has gone though many updates, amendments, and changes over the last few decades.

Most recently, the Fair and Accurate Credit Transaction Act (FACTA) of 2003, added new sections expanding consumer coverage. FACTA permits consumers many rights, including the right to receive a free copy of their credit report each year.

There are also strong regulations on how creditors must deal with identity theft cases, fraud alerts, and how they must dispose of consumer information. Most importantly, the Fair Credit Reporting Act and FACTA allow consumers the right to dispute inaccurate information on their reports.

The exact language reads, *"If the completeness or accuracy of any item of information contained in a consumer's file at a consumer reporting agency is disputed by the consumer and the consumer notifies the agency directly of such dispute, the agency shall reinvestigate free of charge and record the current status of the disputed information, or delete the item from the file in accordance with paragraph (5), before the end of the 30-day period beginning on the date on which the agency receives the notice of the dispute from the consumer."*

There are also many other points and rights presented by the Fair Credit Reporting Act, allowing consumers to challenge the validity of their reports. Once challenged, it then becomes the creditor's responsibility by law to respond to and validate those disputes. This law, this language, and consumer rights to challenge their credit reports are the foundation of credit repair.

Credit Repair Effectiveness

"Credit repair doesn't work," this statement is almost like an urban myth now. Please stop believing it. At the end of the day, Creditors spend millions-of-dollars each year trying to convince consumers just like you that there is nothing you can do to repair your credit.

As a result, most people have heard that credit repair doesn't work at all. This is exactly what the creditors and the bureaus want you to believe, so you don't even try to dispute your inaccurate accounts. But the truth is radically different than the myth. The truth is, credit repair is the most effective way you can actually repair your own credit.

The Credit Repair Secret

Credit repair is extremely effective. But results will vary GREATLY, based on your knowledge and your methodology of how you dispute. If you just mail letters to the credit bureaus not understanding their OCR and E-Oscar computers, your results will not be very good.

The same applies if you dispute online with the credit bureaus. If you take this step, your results again won't be very good. This is one of the main issues with credit repair effectiveness--the repair isn't done properly.

There are a lot of dos and don'ts you will learn, and I want to share the knowledge you need to access the most advanced dispute tactics. If you follow this system, you should be able to have your erroneous, inaccurate, and unverifiable information removed from your credit reports.

What Makes Credit Repair Effective

In the past, credit repair methods included overloading the credit bureaus with letters. The hope was to mail lots of disputes to the bureaus, confuse the person entering the disputes, hope the creditor doesn't respond in time, and the item gets removed.

These types of methods are rarely effective anymore. Even if items get deleted, they are usually put back on the credit report shortly thereafter. This is because the creditor has 30 days to respond to the dispute. If they don't respond, the item gets deleted. But even if they respond 60 days later, the item can legally be put back on the report.

To effectively and permanently delete negative credit items, you must ensure the item gets deleted because the creditor or credit bureaus made mistakes or can't verify the item. You can also have items deleted by indirect dispute methods which are my favorite and I deem them most effective when combined with dispute letters. Then the item will be deleted and stay permanently off your report.

The credit bureaus have gotten much smarter over the years. Most of the dispute process is now automated through two computer systems the credit bureaus use. These computers are the key to success in the dispute process, so understanding them is very important.

OCR

OCR is the first line of defense the credit bureaus use against your disputes. OCR stands for Optical Character Recognition and is used to read every dispute letter you send into the credit bureaus. The computer basically reads your dispute to uncover several things. First, it attempts to see if the dispute is legitimate or what they call frivolous.

The system also automatically categorizes the disputes and flags disputes, creating stall tactics if they feel you are actually trying to improve your credit instead of just disputing one account you might have a question on.

OCR also stores these disputes in a detailed database and auto categorizes disputes with a dispute reason code. This way, you can't dispute again for that same reason or it will not be investigated and instead called "frivolous".

OCR is designed to reduce credit bureau human error and to ensure your disputes are stalled or voided at any chance it gets. It will even read your letters, including the font, paper, color of font, spelling, and other variables to try to see if you have used that letter before, OR if you are using a template letter to dispute.

If OCR thinks you are using a template letter which has been used before or sees another dispute for the same account with a similar reason, it marks it as frivolous and won't investigate the dispute. If it does accept your dispute letter, it auto categorizes and processes the dispute with no human intervention.

This is EXACTLY why you NEVER want to dispute online. Part of the success of disputing is to create confusion with the creditors and the bureaus. When you dispute online, you remove humans from the process. This makes it much easier for that dispute to be validated and for the item to remain on your report.

Disputing online is basically making it easier for OCR. The credit bureaus love it, which is why they make it so convenient for you. But your results will substantially suffer, and your results will be much worse if disputing online.

OCR is also the reason you don't want to just send in letters to the credit bureau, not knowing what you are doing. If you dispute for a similar reason twice, the item is then listed as frivolous, making it very hard to dispute again. The same applies if you are using a common dispute letter or a credit repair company who doesn't custom tailor their disputes.

If OCR picks up these things, your dispute results will suffer greatly. It will then make it much harder to ever get those items deleted.

Success with OCR

Some of our company dispute letters look like they were done by kindergartners. Yes, we do even use crayons and markers to write out some letters. We ALWAYS misspell words and enter some sentences that make no sense. We even dispute in Spanish and French when we can.

You want to use any method you can use to confuse OCR and get your disputes in front of an actual person. There are many ways you can accomplish this.

One of the first successful methods you can use is to do your disputes on heavy stock paper. Using "card stock" paper is a great method because OCR cannot be fed this thickness of paper. In using this paper, you almost automatically get your disputes in front of a human being.

ALWAYS change your fonts on your letters if typing them out and change the color of your fonts. Make sure you misspell words so the disputes don't look like they are coming from a professional credit repair company. And enter wording and sentences that don't make sense, in an attempt to confuse OCR.

It is always a great idea to hand-write your dispute letters. This is one of the best proven methods to get your letters to bypass OCR. In hand-writing your letters, there are several other methods you can use to get past OCR. Use markers and crayons to do the disputes. You can also use pen and pencil, but make sure you misspell words and add sentences that don't make sense.

That is your main goal in disputing to the credit bureaus, bypass OCR, and get your letters in front of a human being for maximum success.

e-OSCAR

e-OSCAR (*Online Solution for Complete and Accurate Reporting*) is the web based automated dispute system used by all three credit bureaus. This is the computer where the credit bureaus input disputes and those disputes are then delivered to the Data Furnisher or creditor who the dispute is for.

Again, the success in disputing has mostly been human confusion and error. e-OSCAR is one more way the credit bureaus automate the process to eliminate human error. e-OSCAR reads your dispute and assigns a 2-digit reason code. This reason code is the reason for the dispute, i.e, the account is not yours, you were never late, etc.

This code is the ONLY content that is pulled out of your letters, and the only content your creditors and the bureaus care about. They look at what account you are disputing and why or the reason for the dispute.

It doesn't matter if your letter comes from an attorney or a personalized sob story to the credit bureaus. OCR or a human at the credit bureaus gets your letter and only enters the REASON for your dispute in a 2 digit code format.

This is the only information the creditor then sees. They know the account that is being disputed, the consumer who is disputing it, and the 2 character reason code for why the account is being disputed.

The creditor then validates the account as accurate, acknowledges that it is incorrect and deletes, or doesn't respond at all within 30 days and the credit bureaus delete. Again, all the creditor has to do is verify they account on their end and in one click validate the item, if accurate.

With the use of e-OSCAR documentation supporting your case, isn't even sent to the creditor. There have even been court cases against the credit bureau in this matter, due to their complete lack of real investigation into the process.

In those cases, *Cushman vs Trans Union* and *Stevenson v. Trans Union* to name two, the credit bureaus lost due to them basically copying the creditor's information instead of actually investigating.

This E-Oscar automation eliminates most of the actual investigation altogether, and most human errors on both the credit bureau and creditor sides are also eliminated.

Success with e-OSCAR

The best way to be successful with e-OSCAR is to use the methods mentioned in the prior Success with OCR section. These methods will get your information past OCR into a human's hands. The "investigator" will then input the information manually into e-OSCAR, which is your first window for an error to be made, and you're the closest you will come to an actual and real dispute.

You might also want to consider disputing multiple erroneous, inaccurate, and unverifiable accounts all at once. If the dispute is handled by a human, this method should increase the probability of a deletion.

Chapter 7
How to Dispute Inaccurate Accounts

It is reported that at least 73% of all credit reports have errors. Rarely have I ever reviewed a report with a client where we didn't locate erroneous or false reporting accounts. Most "mistakes" are mistakes that will count against you, mistakes that hurt your credit, and none were "mistakes" that actually help you.

Before you go acknowledging the reporting of negative accounts on your report as correct, you need to first understand the laws of the Fair Credit Reporting Act. I suggested your order and review his report do an item by item review. You will be shocked at what is on your actual report when you review the details. You will discover that several of those items have incorrect reporting.

On a quick glance, those would be overlooked. And once they are recognized, still many don't know the huge score impact those small "mistakes" make to their credit scores. Dates-of-last activity and dates-of-default drastically affect the credit score and the statute-of-limitations on how long the creditor can pursue you for the debt.

Misreported balances on old collections which are falsely high, or high-credit-limits which are reported lower than they should be, have a very adverse affect on your scores, also. And duplicate accounts reporting means you get the same debt counted against you twice.

When you take a closer detailed review of your report you will most definitely find plenty of mistakes, and when disputed, most of those accounts will be completely deleted. Remember, you are the only one in the credit system who benefits by your credit profiles being good and accurate. If you review your reports, you will most likely find minor inaccuracies that have a significant negative effect on your credit scores.

The Fair Credit Reporting Act gives you the right to dispute inaccurate items on your report. Don't forget this law was founded due to blatant dishonesty and miss-use of consumer information by the credit bureaus. And the bureaus have all been sued or charged since for violating those laws.

All this mean you are the only one who can and will get involved to improve your credit, and disputing is how you can do it. Your disputing should start by sending opt out letters to the indirect third-party credit bureaus- like ARS, INNOVUS via their sister company SageStream, and LEXIS NEXIS. After you have completed all the appropriate opt-outs and suppressions with these parties, then you will start sending letters directly to all three credit bureaus.

The end of this chapter contains some dispute letters based on different reasons which might pertain to your situations. You should start your disputes by finding the errors on your reports and the reasons those items are not accurate. Then you can use or modify any of the letters in this chapter to fit your individual needs.

2nd and 3rd Party Bureaus and Opt-Outs

In this section I want to discuss the secondary credit bureaus that collect various data. These bureaus include ID Analytics and

Sagestream report, Innovis, and Lexis Nexis. You will want to freeze or suppress these reports with these bureaus to make your disputing easier as you move forward. Freezing these reports will make it harder for the credit bureaus to verify any data when it comes to disputing any information.

To remove public records i.e. Tax liens, judgments, and bankruptcies, you must contact the following third-party reporting agencies and have your consumer files frozen. You also should suppress files as well, especially with LexisNexis. With LexisNexis, there is an option to freeze your report but freezing the report will only remove you from online marketing and reporting. You will need to suppress this file which is an extra step. First, I recommend calling to request your free Full File Disclosure and then request suppression of the file.

Note: *All files must have a credit freeze prior to getting a bankruptcy, tax lien or judgment removed. The* **609 letters** *can be used to remove theses public records that are reporting on the 3 credit bureaus. You can also use the* **public record removal letter** *for this type of account public record accounts*

Innovis Security Freeze Options

1-800-540-2505

https://www.innovis.com/securityFreeze/index

Advance Resolution Services(A.R.S.)

1-800-392-8911 (no website)

Advanced Resolution Services, Inc.
5005 Rockside Road, Suite 600

Independence, Ohio 44131

Sagestream (formerly ID Analytics)

1-888-395-0277

SageStream, LLC Consumer Office
P. O. Box 503793
San Diego, CA 92150
https://www.sagestreamllc.com/security-freeze/

LexisNexis

1-888-497-9172

https://www.lexisnexis.com/privacy/

Example of Freeze Request Letters

[Date]

3rd Party Bureau Name
ADDRESS

I wish to freeze my credit report with your company immediately.

Thank you,

(Signature)

72 / Bianca Jules

Name
Address
Ph
SS#
DOB:
Enclosed: Copy of DL and SS card attached

Dispute Reason Codes

We discussed e-OSCAR reason codes in the prior chapter. Each dispute must be for a different reason, or the credit bureaus will mark it as frivolous and not investigate your dispute. FACTA does allow the credit bureaus to ignore frivolous disputes, so you want to use the letters we outline and don't dispute the same account for the same reason.

For example, you can dispute Capital One due to it not being your account. But then your next dispute should be for something different, like that you never paid it late. And your next dispute should be yet for another reason, like the account number is incorrect. Of course, make sure you're disputing legitimate reasons the account might be incorrect.

If you don't change reasons, the credit bureaus might return your dispute as frivolous. This would then waste a lot of time and reduce your chances of being able to successfully dispute and delete in the future. This is one of the many reasons you don't want to just blindly send letters into the credit bureaus. If you do this, in many cases you actually ruin your chances of getting the item deleted the right way.

My research has shown approximately 27 reason codes for the credit bureaus. These are 2-character codes for the different "reasons" you are disputing the account. The letters we provide you include separate reasons for the dispute. This way, each dispute is for a different reason, is assessed a different reason code by e-OSCAR, and this insures your disputes won't be labeled as frivolous.

How Many Accounts to Dispute?

Many consumers wonder if they should dispute only a few of their negative items or all of them. I have found that you can dispute up to 22 accounts on one dispute letter that you find to be inaccurate, unverifiable, or erroneous.

Remember, OCR usually inputs the disputes into the e-OSCAR computer. If you are using the tactics I advise with OCR, your disputes might even get input by a human at the credit bureaus, allowing the possibility for more errors.

Either OCR or a human will pull your dispute out because you dispute too many accounts. In both cases, the goal is just to get the disputes in the system fast so they can quickly get forwarded to the creditor.

So even though OCR or a human bureau investigator will see your dispute letters, your letters won't be stopped if you are disputing multiple accounts at once. Those disputes, once entered into e-OSCAR, get sent to the creditors individually. So your creditors won't know either that you are disputing all your accounts at once.

For this reason, you should consider disputing five or more accounts with each round of disputes. You can even include those disputed accounts on the same dispute letter you mail to the credit bureaus. By disputing more accounts with each round, you will see results much faster.

Since you don't lose any effectiveness with multiple accounts being disputed, consider doing this with each round you dispute. Always try to dispute 5 or more accounts with each round of disputes. You can put all these on the same dispute letter, so don't waste your time completing separate letters for each disputed item. Dispute multiple accounts on the same letter and you will still see very nice results.

What to Include with Your Dispute Letters

There are several things you want to insure are included in every dispute letter you send. Make sure every dispute letter contains the accurate spelling of your first and last name. You should also include your social security number and current home address.

The credit bureaus will NOT dispute unless they KNOW it is you doing the disputing. Your social security number is the main way the bureaus link your disputes to your credit report. This means you must clearly identify yourself in your letter, with your social security number provided.

The credit bureaus will also require you to supply supporting documentation verifying your identity. They want to see your Driver's License and Social Security Card. They will NOT investigate your disputes without this supporting documentation, so include it with each round of disputes.

If you don't have a driver's license, include another legal form of ID. This can include a passport or state ID. If you don't have a Social Security card, provide another form of ID with your social security number on it.

Insure that you do supply a picture ID and a document verifying your social security number to ensure your disputes are investigated properly and quickly.

You should also include the account name and account number on the dispute letter. List the creditor's name and the account number they are reporting to the credit bureau. Sometimes creditors report separate account numbers to each bureau. Look at each account number for each credit bureau you are disputing. Make sure you have that creditor's account number correct on your dispute letter.

Section 609 Dispute Letters

When it comes to section 609 Affidavit dispute, these letters are the most to- the- point method of dispute that covers all types of derogatory accounts. Section 609 of the Fair Credit and Reporting Act, simply puts the onus of verification on the credit bureaus themselves. Since the original law was put into effect prior to the electronic and computer digital age, it was revised to meet current technology standards. The current version of the FCRA now requires the credit bureaus to have physical copies in their files of documentation to support each account being reported on your file. The fact is that creditors actually report all of your credit items to the credit bureaus electronically and never send any type of physical document to the credit bureaus. In turn, none of the credit bureaus review or verify any signed contract, any credit applications or ANY document before it is reported on your credit report. Keep these facts in mind as this knowledge is what you are able to use to your advantage as to why any and all items can be removed legally from your report. The section 609 is written in favor of the consumer that will help aid you in deleting any derogatory information and can be upheld in any court if you use these letters correctly.

When you study this Federal Law and any case laws established in various court cases pertaining to the FCRA, it will be a common thread that the FCRA requires that all credit reporting agencies are supposed to VERIFY all information they receive from creditors Before this information is added to your credit file. In actuality, the credit bureaus carry out this process in reverse and only seek to verify any information through a digital code and only AFTER a consumer dispute is made. Further, an electronic code is not proper verification of a creditor item. They are required to have physical proof in their files to show that they have verified the information and that the account does indeed belong to you as the consumer.

The subsection (2)(E) of 609 states "...whereby, "accurate" derogatory information can be removed. 2.) The information cannot be verified. The term "verification" is the focus point of the entire deletion process.

The credit reporting agencies being required by law to verify the credit information and not the creditor. With this face, anything that is included in your credit report file can be removed if you request the credit reporting bureaus right to report an item by demanding that they show you proof of verification that should be in the bureaus files. Essentially, you can effectively remove any negative valid and invalid item through this method of section 609 dispute letters.

The fact is that the credit bureaus have intentionally chosen NOT to verify your accounts in the manner that the FCRA law was written. They will also try all kinds of intimidation tactics through their response letters in efforts to discourage you from continuing your disputes. DO NOT BE DETERRED by the various "form letters" or receiving various communication letters that you may receive from the bureaus.

These letters may range from asking you if you are doing business with a credit repair company, request that you fill out a questionnaire and return it to them before they will review your dispute, or send you letters claiming your letters as suspicious, or deem your dispute letter as "frivolous". They receive thousands of letters per day and they will try all kinds of intimidation tactics to scare you away or discourage you. Please be advised DO NOT FILL OUT ANY FORM LETTER that they request you fill out to return to them. If you receive any rejection letters or intimidation letter, move forward with sending the next letter and remind them it is your 2nd request! Keep the letters moving forward.

FCRA Section 610(a)(1) [§ 1681h] states that a credit bureau is only required to respond to a dispute from a consumer, if it is in writing and if the consumer properly verifies their identity with proper identification.

Mailing Your Section 609 Dispute Letter

Note #1: As mentioned in earlier chapters, you will want to remove all duplicate name variations and past addresses. If there are current positive tradelines that are reporting with old addresses, you will want to contact the positive creditors only and update with new address that is not associated with any negative account. You can get new address from UPS or ipostal.com that report as actual street addresses. Get this address updated on your driver's license. Refer to Chapter 4 for the previous details for updating this section.

If you do not have a copy of your SSN card, a copy of a pay stub or W-2 form that shows your name and SSN will suffice. Below is an example of personal letter to update and remove any variations of names and addresses.

PERSONAL IDENTITY SECTION UPDATE LETTER

Date
Name
Address
SS#:
Date of Birth

BUREAU
ADDRESS

In reviewing a copy of my recent credit report, I discovered it contained some errors pertaining to the following "Personal Information." Due to the FCRA 15 USC 1681 et seq. I am disputing all inaccurate information that does not correspond with my state issued documentation. Please report the date accurately to remove any inaccurate information from my report. Please find attached my Drivers License and SS Card. Please kindly **UPDATE** and **AMEND** your records to reflect my **CORRECT** identification.

For the record, this tis the ONLY correct information that should be on my profile:

My name is:
DOB:
Address:
Employer:

Please **REMOVE** all other inaccurate name variations as it is inconsistent with my documented identity.
(list name variations)

Also, my current address is: *(current address)*
Please **REMOVE** all other inaccurate address:

(List all old addresses here...)

Please send me notification that these items have been deleted, as well as updated. If not removed I will contact the FTC and matters within my legal rights to correct my profile as your ill reporting is hindering my financial profile.

* Please remove all **non-account holding inquiries** over 30 days old.
* Please add a **Promotional Suppression** to my credit file.

Thank You,
{YOUR NAME HERE}

```
┌─────────────────────────────┐
│                             │
│                             │
│      COPY OF ID CARD        │
│                             │
│  (Driver's License, Passport or │
│         State ID Card)      │
│                             │
│                             │
├─────────────────────────────┤
│                             │
│                             │
│                             │
│      COPY of SSN CARD       │
│                             │
│                             │
│                             │
└─────────────────────────────┘
```

Note # 2: With each Section 609 Dispute Letters, you will include a notarized copy of your driver's license and/or a picture ID card, or a picture ID card and a copy of your Social Security Card. Make sure that the address showing on your driver license is the same address showing on your credit report.

Note # 3 Also be sure to handwrite the envelopes, and do not type them. Handwriting the letters will ensure that the workers who deal with the incoming dispute letters will not have the time to adequately process the letters because when the OCR cannot read the letters, they are placed in a manual file. The workers have a strict quota and usually the "manual stack" of handwritten letters have a 50/50 chance of being placed in the "verified" form letter file or the delete all disputed line items because the workers are behind on the manual stack of handwritten letters. Since they only have 30 days to process disputes, the workers often don't have time to process every dispute.

Note # 4: During the entire dispute process, it is recommended to NOT apply for any additional credit during the dispute process and do not allow anyone to pull your credit during this time either... Only unless it is necessary. Also, during the dispute process, it is critical to not speak to any debt collectors over the phone. Only communicate with any collection creditor during this time in writing. Communicating only in writing will increase your chances that you will be able to get rid of the particular outstanding debt without getting sued or having to pay anything back.

Note #5: When you begin the actual mailing of the letters, you will want to be sure to stagger your mailing of dispute letters between each bureau of at least 4 days before mailing the next letter to the 2nd credit bureau and then another 4 days before mailing to the 3rd bureau.

Note #6: Another key to getting success from your section 609 affidavit dispute letters is to bypass the OCR system. One way to effectively do this is to handwrite sections of your letters and handwrite your social security number in your heading. I would try different tactics if you also have particularly neat handwriting like inserting any keyboard symbol into the last 4 digits of your SSN. You can also alternate handwriting in the name of the account and the account number onto the letter. The point to this is to get your letter read by an actual live person which will increase the chances of getting the negative item removed on the first or 2nd letter. When filing out the account section of the letter, it is ok to enter the partial account numbers for each account you want deleted. In the column for Provide Physical Verification, you want to input "Unverified Account".

Note #7: Each letter you will need to have notarized and signed. Be sure to make copy of ALL your letters prior to mailing for your records and mail them Certified Mail. Making copies will ensure that you have established proof of your paper trail. Mailing certified will also serve to track the delivery receipt of the letters if they were received by the Credit Bureau agency. If the credit bureau ends up not responding or ignoring your letters by doing nothing or no response, they will be forced to delete all items requested when shown to them or if you must prove in small claims court.

Note #8: Do not be afraid to take to small claims court if need at the end of all dispute letters. Remember the FCRA is your favor as the consumer for your protection the way the section 609 is written. Small claims court is one of the easiest to file. Credit Bureaus do not want matters to go to public courts and run the risk of having the masses discover truths of FCRA and how the credit bureaus are not following the FCRA by not actually verifying any creditor accounts nor providing documentation upon request. They would not want to risk case law being established in open court and the public and putting a dark cloud over their reputable reputation. However, you can use this knowledge to challenge their "right to report" and get your derogatory accounts removed. Once a valid section 609 dispute letter is received, the credit bureaus when properly challenged comply without further resistance.

Below I have outlined the rounds of dispute letters for Section 609. The letters will need to be individually addressed to each bureau address and staggered mailing as described above. I have also included additional mailing addresses for the credit bureaus for reference.

TransUnion
P.O. Box 6790
Fullerton, CA 92834

TRANSUNION
FRAUD Victim Assistance Dept
P.O. Box 6790 , Fullerton, CA 92634-6790
TRANSUNION
FRAUD DEPARTMENT
P.O. Box 34012
Fullerton, CA 92834

EXPERIAN
P.O. Box 9530
Allen, TX 75013

EXPERIAN
P.O. Box 4500
Allen, TX 75013

Experian
National Consumer Assistance
P.O. Box 2104
Allen, TX 75013
1-888-397-3742

Experian
P.O.Box
Allen, TX. 75013

EQUIFAX
P.O. BOX 740241
ATLANTA, GA 30374

EQUIFAX

Fraud Assistance
P.O. Box 105069
Atlanta, GA 30348
1-404-885-8000
1-800-525-6285
FAX: 1-770-375-2821

Letter ROUND #1

January 1, 2016

Your Name
Address
City, State Zip
SSN: 000-00-0000 | DOB: 1/1/1970

BUREAU
ADDRESS

According to the Fair Credit Reporting Act, **Section 609 (a)(1)(A), you are required by federal law to verify** - through the physical verification of the original signed consumer contract - any and all accounts you post on a credit report. Otherwise, anyone paying for your reporting services could fax, mail or email in a fraudulent account.

I demand to see Verifiable Proof (**an original Consumer Contract with my Signature on it**) you have on file of the accounts listed below. Your failure to positively verify these accounts has hurt my ability to obtain credit. Under the FCRA, unverified accounts must be removed and if you are unable to provide me a copy of verifiable proof, you must remove the accounts listed below.

I demand the following accounts be verified or removed immediately.

Name of Account	Account Number	Provide Physical Verification
Creditor 1	1234567890	Unverified Account
Creditor 2	etc	Unverified Account
Creditor 3		Unverified Account
Creditor 4		Unverified Account
Creditor 5		Unverified Account
Creditor 6.		Unverified Account
	HANDWRITE THIS SECTION	
Creditor 7		Unverified Account
Creditor 8		Unverified Account
Creditor 9		Unverified Account
Creditor 10		Unverified Account
Creditor 11		Unverified Account
Creditor 12		Unverified Account
Creditor 13		Unverified Account
Creditor 14		Unverified Account
Creditor 15		Unverified Account
Creditor 16		Unverified Account
Creditor 17		Unverified Account
Creditor 18		Unverified Account
Creditor 19		Unverified Account
Creditor 20		Unverified Account
Creditor 21		Unverified Account
Creditor 22		Unverified Account

Thank You, {YOUR NAME HERE}

IN WITNESS WHEREOF, the said party has signed and sealed these presents the day and year first above written.

Signed, sealed and delivered in the presence of: {PRINT YOUR NAME HERE}

_____

Signature

STATE OF
COUNTY OF

I HEREBY CERTIFY that on this day before me, an officer duly qualified to take acknowledgments, personally appeared { YOUR NAME HERE }, who is personally known to me o who has produced _____ as identificati on an who executed the foregoing instrument and he/she acknowledged before me that he/she execute the same.

WITNESS my hand and official seal in the County and State aforesaid this _____ day of _____ 2016.

Notary Public
Printed Name: _____

My commission expires:

COPY of SSN CARD

COPY OF ID CARD

(Driver's License, Passport or State ID Card)

Letter ROUND #2

January 1, 2016

Your Name
Address
City, State Zip
SSN: 000-00-0000 | DOB: 1/1/1970

BUREAU
ADDRESS

Please be advised this is my SECOND WRITTEN REQUEST. The unverified items listed below remain on credit report in violation of Federal Law. You are required under the FCRA to have a copy of the original credit documentation on file to verify that this information is mine and is correct. In the results of your first investiga you stated in writing that you **"verified"** that these items are being **"reported correctly"** ? Who verified th accounts?

You have **NOT** provided me a copy of ANY original documentation required under **Section 609 (a)(1)(A)** **Section 611 (a)(1)(A)** (a consumer contract with my signature on it) and under **Section 611 (5)(A)** of the F you are required to **"...promptly DELETE all information which cannot be verified."**

The law is very clear as to the Civil liability and the remedy available to me for "negligent noncomplia **Section 617**) if you fail to comply. **I am a litigious consumer and fully intend on pursuing litigation in matter to enforce my rights under the FCRA**

demand the following accounts be deleted immediately.

Name of Account	Account Number	Provide Physical Verification
Creditor 1	1234567890	Unverified Account
Creditor 2	etc	Unverified Account
Creditor 3		Unverified Account
Creditor 4		Unverified Account
Creditor 5		Unverified Account
Creditor 6.		Unverified Account
	HANDWRITE THIS SECTION	
Creditor 7		Unverified Account
Creditor 8		Unverified Account
Creditor 9		Unverified Account
Creditor 10		Unverified Account
Creditor 11		Unverified Account
Creditor 12		Unverified Account
Creditor 13		Unverified Account
Creditor 14		Unverified Account
Creditor 15		Unverified Account
Creditor 16		Unverified Account
Creditor 17		Unverified Account
Creditor 18		Unverified Account
Creditor 19		Unverified Account
Creditor 20		Unverified Account
Creditor 21		Unverified Account
Creditor 22		Unverified Account

Thank You,{YOUR NAME HERE}

IN WITNESS WHEREOF, the said party has signed and sealed these presents the day and year first above written.

Signed, sealed and delivered in the presence of: {PRINT YOUR NAME HERE}

_____

Signature

STATE OF
COUNTY OF

I HEREBY CERTIFY that on this day before me, an officer duly qualified to take acknowledgments, personally appeared { YOUR NAME HERE }, who is personally known to me or who has produced _____ as identification and who executed the foregoing instrument and he/she acknowledged before me that he/she executed the same.

WITNESS my hand and official seal in the County and State aforesaid this _____ day of _____ 2016.

_____

Notary Public
Printed Name:
                    My commission expires:

```
┌─────────────────────────────┐
│                             │
│      COPY of SSN CARD       │
│                             │
└─────────────────────────────┘
```

```
┌─────────────────────────────┐
│                             │
│       COPY OF ID CARD       │
│                             │
│   (Driver's License, Passport or │
│         State ID Card)      │
└─────────────────────────────┘
```

Letter ROUND #3

January 1, 2016

Your Name
Address
City, State Zip
SSN: 000-00-0000 | DOB: 1/1/1970

BUREAU
ADDRESS

Please be advised this is my THIRD WRITTEN REQUEST and FINAL WARNING that I fully intend to pursue litigation in accordance with the FCRA to enforce my rights and seek relief and recover all monetary damages that I may be entitled to under Section 616 and Section 617 regarding your continued willful and negligent noncompliance.

Despite my previous two written requests, the below mentioned unverified items remain on my credit report in violation of Federal Law. You are required under the FCRA to have a copy of the original creditors documentation on file to verify that this information is mine and is correct. In the results of your first investigation and subsequent reinvestigation, you stated in writing that you **"verified"** that these items are being **"reported correctly"** ? Who verified these accounts? You have **NOT** provided me a copy of ANY original documentation (a consumer contract with my signature on it) as required under **Section 609 (a)(1) & Section 611 (a)(1)(A).** Furthermore you have failed to provide the method of verification as required under Section 611 (a) (7). Please be advised that under **Section 611 (5)(A)** of the FCRA – you are required to *"…promptly DELETE all information which cannot be verified."*

The law is very clear as to the Civil liability and the remedy available to me (**Section 616 & 617**) if you fail to comply with Federal Law. I am a litigious consumer and fully intend on pursuing litigation in this matter to enforce my rights under the FCRA.

I demand the following accounts be deleted immediately.

Name of Account	Account Number	Provide Physical Verification
Creditor 1	1234567890	Unverified Account
Creditor 2	etc	Unverified Account
Creditor 3		Unverified Account
Creditor 4		Unverified Account
Creditor 5		Unverified Account
Creditor 6.		Unverified Account
	HANDWRITE THIS SECTION	
Creditor 7		Unverified Account
Creditor 8		Unverified Account
Creditor 9		Unverified Account
Creditor 10		Unverified Account
Creditor 11		Unverified Account
Creditor 12		Unverified Account
Creditor 13		Unverified Account
Creditor 14		Unverified Account
Creditor 15		Unverified Account
Creditor 16		Unverified Account
Creditor 17		Unverified Account
Creditor 18		Unverified Account
Creditor 19		Unverified Account
Creditor 20		Unverified Account
Creditor 21		Unverified Account
Creditor 22		Unverified Account

IN WITNESS WHEREOF, the said party has signed and sealed these presents the day and year first above written.

Signed, sealed and delivered in the presence of: {PRINT YOUR NAME HERE}

_____

                    Signature

STATE OF
COUNTY OF

I HEREBY CERTIFY that on this day before me, an officer duly qualified to take acknowledgments, personally appeared { YOUR NAME HERE }, who is personally known to me o who has produced _____ as identificati on an(who executed the foregoing instrument and he/she acknowledged before me that he/she execute the same.

WITNESS my hand and official seal in the County and State aforesaid this _____ day of _____ 2016.

_____

Notary Public
Printed Name:

                    My commission expires:

COPY of SSN CARD

COPY OF ID CARD

(Driver's License, Passport or State ID Card)

Letter ROUND #4:

DATE

Your Name
Address
City, State Zip
SSN: 000-00-0000 | DOB: 1/1/1970

BUREAU
ADDRESS

NOTICE OF PENDING LITIGATION SEEKING RELIEF AND MONETARY DAMAGES UNDER FCRA SECTION 616 & SECTION 617

Please accept this final written **OFFER OF SETTLEMENT BEFORE LITIGATION** as my attempt to amicably resolve your continued violation of the Fair Credit Reporting Act regarding your refusal to delete **UNVERIFIED information from my consumer file.** I intend to pursue litigation in accordance with FCRA to seek relief and recover all monetary damages that I may be entitled to under Section 616 and Section 617 if the UNVERIFIED items listed below are not deleted immediately. A copy of this letter as well as copies of the three written letters sent to you previously will also become part of a formal complaint to the Federal Trade Commission and shall be used as evidence in pending litigation provided you fail to comply with this offer of settlement.

Despite three written requests, the unverified items listed below still remain on my credit report in violation of Federal Law. You are required under the FCRA to have a copy of the original creditors documentation on file to verify that this information is mine and is correct. In the results of your investigations, you stated in writing that you **"verified"** that these items are being **"reported correctly"?** Who verified these accounts? You have **NOT** provided me a copy of ANY original documentation (a consumer contract with my signature on it) as required under **Section 609 (a)(1)(A) & Section 611 (a)(1)(A).** Furthermore you have failed to provide the method of verification as required under **Section 611 (a) (7).** Please be advised that under **Section 611 (5)** of the FCRA – you are required to **"...promptly DELETE all information which cannot be verified."**

The law is very clear as to the Civil liability and the remedy available to me (**Section 616 & 617**) if you fail to comply with Federal Law. I am a litigious consumer and fully intend on pursuing litigation in this matter to enforce my rights under the FCRA.

I demand the following accounts be verified or deleted immediately.

Name of Account	Account Number	Provide Physical Verification
Creditor 1	1234567890	Unverified Account
Creditor 2	etc	Unverified Account
Creditor 3		Unverified Account
Creditor 4		Unverified Account
Creditor 5		Unverified Account
Creditor 6.		Unverified Account
	HANDWRITE THIS SECTION	
Creditor 7		Unverified Account
Creditor 8		Unverified Account
Creditor 9		Unverified Account
Creditor 10		Unverified Account
Creditor 11		Unverified Account
Creditor 12		Unverified Account

Thank You, {YOUR NAME HERE}

IN WITNESS WHEREOF, the said party has signed and sealed these presents the day and year first above written.

Signed, sealed and delivered in the presence of: {PRINT YOUR NAME HERE}

_____

Signature

STATE OF
COUNTY OF

I HEREBY CERTIFY that on this day before me, an officer duly qualified to take acknowledgments, personally appeared { YOUR NAME HERE }, who is personally known to me o who has produced _____ as identificati on an(who executed the foregoing instrument and he/she acknowledged before me that he/she execute the same.

WITNESS my hand and official seal in the County and State aforesaid this _____ day of _____ 2016.

Notary Public
Printed Name: _____

My commission expires:

COPY of SSN CARD

COPY OF ID CARD

(Driver's License, Passport or State ID Card)

Alternative Disputing and Finding the Best Dispute Letter to Send

Every credit file is different. And I want to spell out other used dispute letter tactics that have also worked. The main difference with credit bureau dispute letters is the reason in the letter for the dispute. Remember, you must dispute each time for a different reason to avoid the dispute being labeled as frivolous.

Find the best letter for the reason of your disputes. Is the account yours? Did you pay it late? Does the account belong to someone else? There are many reasons on the letters, just pick which one you feel works best for your situation.

If you dispute the account and the creditor verifies that the account is accurately reporting, you will need to dispute again for another reason for something you have found to be done inaccurate.

Remember, you are making the creditor verify the information they are reporting as they are required to do by law. If the creditor doesn't have a record of the account anymore, they won't respond or will tell the credit bureaus that it should be deleted.

If you do CLEARLY know the account is not valid for a particular reason, dispute for that reason and include any supporting documentation you have. This supporting documentation will not be supplied to the creditor with your dispute, but it does help show the credit bureaus that you can prove your case.

Don't be surprised if you dispute an account you KNOW is inaccurate, then see that the account is verified. Keep in mind, the creditor doesn't see the evidence you send in with your disputes. You will need to follow the exact dispute process of opting out, updating your personal information section, and send out a few dispute letters; even direct creditor letters, to see the item get deleted.

It is important to keep disputing for different reasons the account is inaccurate or erroneous until you find a reason they can't verify. If they are verifying the account with these disputes, advanced debt validation techniques should then help get those items deleted. You will learn more about these advanced methods in the following chapter.

Complete and Mail Your Dispute Letter

Now you have all the fundamentals in the dispute process. It is time together your disputes and get them in the mail. Sit down with your credit report to review your negative items. You can then log those items in a log for tracking.

Next you will want to choose the best dispute letter. Dispute the reason the account is not accurate, erroneous, or unverifiable. Complete the dispute letter with your account and personal details. Make sure you include your name, address, and your social security number on the dispute letter. Also make sure you sign the letter.

Ensure you complete the creditors' names and account numbers which you are disputing. Make sure you have the correct account number that is listed on your report for the bureau you are disputing. Remember, account numbers might vary between different credit bureaus.

Include your IDs with your letter. They will want to see your Driver's License and Social Security Card. If you don't have those, supply another state or federal picture ID and additional verification of your social security number.

Mail your disputes to each credit bureau. The credit bureau addresses are listed later in this chapter. The first address listed is the primary address for each credit bureau.
There are also many more addresses listed for each bureau. Log the date you mail out your disputes.

Waiting for and Checking Your Results

It will take between 30-45 days for you to receive results. In many cases, it will take 40-45 days. Sometimes you will receive results faster but expect to see them after 40 days. If they do arrive early, you can then be pleasantly surprised.

The Fair and Accurate Credit Transaction Act gives the creditor 30 days to respond to the dispute. This means they have 30 days from the date the dispute is entered by the credit bureaus into e-OSCAR.

You should allow time for the disputes to get mailed to the credit bureau and allow for some time for the bureaus to initiate the dispute. Therefore 40-45 days is a good expectant time-frame to wait for your results.

FACTA requires the credit bureaus to respond to you by mail with your results ONLY if you request they do so in writing. Ensure that you include a sentence on the credit bureau dispute letter requesting that they reply to your dispute by mail. They then are required by law to mail you back your reports.

The credit bureaus will then send you copies of your credit reports by mail. These reports will come in larger than normal envelopes with only P.O. Boxes in the return address section. You will be able to see your results on the first page of most reports you receive, but each bureau's report looks a little different.

Trans Union

Trans Union reports are very easy to read. Their results are on the first page and appear as a list. The list shows you the account name, account number, and the result. You hope to see Deleted. Sometimes you will see VERIFIED, NO CHANGE and other times you will see NEW INFORMATION BELOW.

When the report shows that new information is on the report, it is usually a minor correction to the reported data. The negative item probably still remains but has been modified. Sometimes this change is the date of last activity, or the balance owed, or whatever other factor you disputed the creditor for.

Trans Union will then give you the account details so you can see what information has been updated and changed. And they will give you access to your online credit report with them. This "backdoor" is very valuable. This is where you can actually see exactly what Trans Union is reporting for you. Sometimes this data isn't 100% accurate through credit monitoring.

But with Trans Union themselves, your credit report is 100% accurate. Check your reports, and enter results per the instructions in the next Track Results section of this guide.

Experian

Your results can be on your Experian reports on page 1 or 2. They also provide you a list summary of your results. This list shows the account name, account number, and status. The status is either "Deleted", "Remains", "Updated", or "Reviewed".

You are shooting for a "Deleted" result. "Remains" is the worst result, as this indicates the item will stay on the report with no change at all. If the account is "Updated," a change was made to the item but it remains on your report.

If you disputed that the item belongs to you, this status will indicate that they verified it does belong to you. If you disputed the account for another reason, review the report for what was changed. "Reviewed" simply means you need to check the report yourself for results. It can indicate either a deletion or update. You won't see too many of this result type.

Experian will provide you other account details in the report they send. These details include the creditor's name, address, and phone number. You will also see the account number and date originally filed. Many other account details and notes on the account are all available on this report.

Equifax

Equifax reports don't really have a good summary section. You will have to review the account details on your report to see what has changed. They do typically show you the update and deleted accounts first on the first two pages of the report. These are under "The Results of Our Investigation," and "Collection Agency."

These sections will tell you the results of the disputes. They will list the creditor's name and account number. They will then tell you in a sentence what the results were. The statuses are much the same as the other credit bureaus. You are striving for a DELETE. They will also UPDATE or VERIFY the account.

If updated, Equifax will tell you in the summary description what exactly was updated. Go through your report item-by-item during your review and highlight all the negative accounts which still remain.

The credit bureau reports give you a lot of additional details you won't find on a credit monitoring report. Review these details thoroughly, as each one is another reason for another dispute. The "Last Reported" with Experian, "Date Paid" with Trans Union, and "Date of 1st Delinquency" with Equifax are VERY important indicators.

All of these indicators reflect the date the account was last used or the last time you made a payment. This date is one of the most important dates on your credit report. This is the date which determines how long the account will stay on your credit report. Most derogatory accounts remain on your credit report for seven years.

The seven years is from the date you last made a payment on that account. This is the same date we are discussing here. This date is very important, as it reflects how long the negative account is due to remain on your report.

Do it Again

Review and log your results. Be sure to make copies of all your dispute letters mailed. Make sure you thoroughly review your reports to make sure that you know of all the negative items that still remain on your reports.

You will probably see a lot of negatives removed with your early disputes. This is because you are narrowing down the creditors who actually have enough information on you to even report the item.

Many creditors keep bad records or delete your records when the account is sold to collections. This means one simple dispute for any reason will remove many of these accounts. You will also have a lot of creditors who verified or updated the account information. These are creditors you will need to continue disputing to get the items removed.

Once you have your log completed with the negative creditors who still remain, complete the steps mentioned above for mailing out another round of credit bureau disputes. Each month you will want to continue disputing to the credit bureaus. After 1-2 rounds of these credit bureau disputes, you will be able to narrow down your real problem creditors.

These are usually the creditors who are reporting the most recent data for you. The more recent a negative item is, the greater chance the creditor has all your information readily available. Those accounts will require more dispute work from you to have them removed.

After your first or second round of disputes, you will also want to start some of your Advanced Dispute tactics discussed in the next chapter. With both your credit bureau and direct creditor disputing going simultaneously, you will see more success in deleting your recent and more harmful accounts. Still, start with credit bureau disputes to narrow down the creditors who are really going to cause you problems.

Every time you receive results from the credit bureaus, do your review, log your results, and then initiate another round of credit bureau disputes. If you don't receive your reports back from the credit bureaus, review your updated report with your credit monitoring service.

One of the new credit bureau stall tactics is to not even send back the reports to you. After 40 days pass with no results received in the mail, login to your credit monitoring account to see the changes. You will typically find that the credit bureaus did to the investigation and update your results; they just didn't mail the results back.

If this happens, use your updated credit report through the monitoring service to track your results. You will then log your result and send out another round of disputes for the negative accounts that still remain on your reports.

Sample Dispute Letters

This section has 10 dispute letters which will help you during the dispute process. Locate the letter which best addresses the reason you feel your account is inaccurate.

Or you can modify these letters with a reason which better fits why the account is inaccurate.

Sample Letter 1- I do not recognize this creditor

Credit Bureau Name							Your Name

Credit Bureau Address						Your Address

Credit Bureau City, State, and Zip			Your City, State, Zip

											Your Date of Birth

Date										Your Social Security Number

Dear CREDIT BUREAU NAME,

Re: Account Name and Number

I am contacting you because I have found some information that is inaccurate on my credit report.

I do not recognize this creditor on my report at all. I request that you verify the information and remove any inaccurate information from my credit report as quickly as possible. The items in question are:

CREEDITORS NAME AND ACCOUNT NUMBER

After doing so please provide me with an updated credit report reflecting the changes.

Thank you for your time,

YOUR SIGNATURE, YOUR FIRST AND LAST NAME

Sample Letter 2- Outdated Information Reported

Credit Bureau Name	Your Name
Credit Bureau Address	Your Address
Credit Bureau City, State, and Zip	Your City, State, Zip
	Your Date of Birth
Date	Your Social Security Number

Dear CREDIT BUREAU NAME,

Re: Account Name and Number

This letter is a formal request to remove outdated information from my credit report. For easy reference, I've listed the items below which are outdated.

INSERT ACCOUNT DETAILS HERE

In accordance with the Fair Credit Reporting Act, Section 605 [15 U.S.C. § 1681c] "Running of Reporting Period", as of December 29, 1997, reporting periods only run 7 or 10 years depending on the type of information. In my case, the information in question expired as of [insert date].

I respectfully ask you to investigate my claim and if you find my claim to be valid then I expect you to immediately remove the outdated items identified in this letter and any additional outdated items that you discover during your investigation. Furthermore, after correcting my credit file, I request that you forward a corrected copy of my credit report to me at the address listed at the top of this letter.

Finally, if your investigation determines the information is not outdated, I respectfully request you forward to me a description of the procedure used to determine the accuracy and completeness of the item in question. In accordance with the FCRA I respectfully request you forward this information within 15 days of the completion of your re-investigation.

Thank you for your consideration and cooperation in resolving this matter. If you have any questions concerning this issue I can be reached at: {insert daytime phone number including area code).

Sincerely,

Thank you for your time,

YOUR SIGNATURE

YOUR FIRST AND LAST NAME

YOUR SOCIAL SECURITY NUMBER

Sample Letter 3- Incorrect Account Numbers

Credit Bureau Name   Your Name

Credit Bureau Address   Your Address

Credit Bureau City, State, and Zip   Your City, State, Zip

                                        Your Date of Birth

Date   Your Social Security Number

Dear CREDIT BUREAU NAME,

Re: Account Name and Number

I am contacting you because I have found some information that is inaccurate on my credit report.

The account number listed on my report doesn't match any of my records. I request that you verify the information and remove any inaccurate information from my credit report as quickly as possible. The items in question are:

CREEDITORS NAME AND ACCOUNT NUMBER

After doing so please provide me with an updated credit report reflecting the changes.

Thank you for your time,

YOUR SIGNATURE, YOUR FIRST AND LAST NAME

Sample Letter 4- Amount Owed is Incorrect

Credit Bureau Name   Your Name

Credit Bureau Address   Your Address

Credit Bureau City, State, and Zip   Your City, State, Zip

Your Date of Birth

Date   Your Social Security Number

Dear CREDIT BUREAU NAME,

Re: Account Name and Number

I am contacting you because I have found some information that is inaccurate on my credit report.

The amount that is reported I owe is inaccurate as it is reported. I request that you verify the information and remove any inaccurate information from my credit report as quickly as possible. The items in question are:

CREEDITORS NAME AND ACCOUNT NUMBER

After doing so please provide me with an updated credit report reflecting the changes.

Thank you for your time,

YOUR SIGNATURE, YOUR FIRST AND LAST NAME

Sample Letter 5- Incorrect Balance

Credit Bureau Name

Credit Bureau Address

Credit Bureau City, State, and Zip

Date

Your Name

Your Address

Your City, State, Zip

Your Date of Birth

Your Social Security Number

Dear CREDIT BUREAU NAME,

Re: Account Name and Number

I am contacting you because I have found some information that is inaccurate on my credit report.

The balance you are reporting I owe is incorrect, and doesn't match my records. I request that you verify the information and remove any inaccurate information from my credit report as quickly as possible. The items in question are:

CREEDITORS NAME AND ACCOUNT NUMBER

After doing so please provide me with an updated credit report reflecting the changes.

YOUR SIGNATURE, YOUR FIRST AND LAST NAME

Sample Letter 6-General Dispute, Insert Reason

Credit Bureau Name   Your Name

Credit Bureau Address   Your Address

Credit Bureau City, State, and Zip   Your City, State, Zip

                                                                               Your Date of Birth

Date   Your Social Security Number

Dear CREDIT BUREAU NAME,

Re: Account Name and Number

This letter is a formal request to correct inaccurate information contained in my credit file. The item(s) listed below is/are completely (insert appropriate word(s) {inaccurate, incorrect, incomplete, erroneous, misleading, outdated}). I have listed the items below which are incorrect and need to be deleted from my credit file.

Line Item: {insert name of creditor, account number or line item number)

Item Description: (this info is found on your credit report)

In accordance with the federal Fair Credit Reporting Act (FCRA), I respectfully request you investigate my claim and, if after your investigation, you find my claim to be valid and accurate, I request that you immediately {delete, update, correct} the item.

Furthermore, I request that you supply a corrected copy of my credit profile to me and all creditors who have received a copy within the last 6 months, or the last 2 years for employment purposes. Additionally, please provide me with the name, address, and *telephone number of each credit grantor or other subscriber that you provided a copy of my credit report too within the past six months.*

If your investigation shows the information to be accurate, I respectfully request that you forward to me a description of the procedure used to determine the accuracy and completeness of the item in question within 15 days of the completion of your re-investigation as required by the Fair Credit Reporting Act.

I thank you for your consideration and cooperation. If you have any questions concerning this matter I can be reached at (insert daytime phone number including area code).

Thank you for your time,

YOUR SIGNATURE

YOUR FIRST AND LAST NAME

YOUR SOCIAL SECURITY NUMBER

Sample Letter 7- Don't Recognize the Account

Credit Bureau Name

Credit Bureau Address

Credit Bureau City, State, and Zip

Date

Your Name

Your Address

Your City, State, Zip

Your Date of Birth

Your Social Security Number

Dear CREDIT BUREAU NAME,

Re: Account Name and Number

I recently obtained a copy of my credit report, which contains accounts I can't remember ever having! I have no idea what these accounts are and request they be removed. I am NOT claiming fraud or identity theft - I do not honestly remember.

CREDIT ACCOUNT NAME AND ACCOUNT NUMBER

When my credit report has been corrected please send a corrected report to me.

Thank you for your time,

YOUR SIGNATURE, YOUR FIRST AND LAST NAME

Sample Letter 8- Don't Recognize Account

Credit Bureau Name   Your Name

Credit Bureau Address   Your Address

Credit Bureau City, State, and Zip   Your City, State, Zip

                              Your Date of Birth

Date   Your Social Security Number

Dear CREDIT BUREAU NAME,

Re: Account Name and Number

This letter is to request you to remove inaccurate information from my credit report. Such inaccurate information has affected my chances of getting loans and credit. For your convenience, I have supplied a list of inaccurate accounts below.
ENTER ACCOUNT INFORMATION HERE

I hereby request you to make the changes within 30 days so as to avoid any violation of the FCRA. Please send me a copy of the changed credit report at the earliest.

Thank you for your time,

YOUR SIGNATURE, YOUR FIRST AND LAST NAME

Sample Letter 9- Don't Recognize Account

Credit Bureau Name

Credit Bureau Address

Credit Bureau City, State, and Zip

Date

Your Name

Your Address

Your City, State, Zip

Your Date of Birth

Your Social Security Number

Dear CREDIT BUREAU NAME,

Re: Account Name and Number

I recently obtained a copy of my credit report from your service and have found the following items to be in error.

CREDITOR NAME AND ACCOUNT NUMBER

According to Section 611 of the Fair Credit Reporting Act, I am requesting that you
re-investigate those items indicated, and promptly delete any unverifiable, inaccurate, or outdated information from my credit report.
In addition, I am requesting a description of how the investigation was conducted
along with the name, address, and telephone number of anyone contacted for
information. Furthermore, if there is a change in my credit history resulting
from your investigation, I am requesting that an updated report be sent to those
who received my report, within the last two years for employment purposes, or
within the last one year for any other purpose.

Please send me an updated copy of my report, and notification that items have been deleted. I will consider 30 days a reasonable time for your re-verification of
these items.

Thank you for your prompt attention in this matter.

Thank you for your time,

YOUR SIGNATURE

YOUR FIRST AND LAST NAME

YOUR SOCIAL SECURITY NUMBER

Sample Letter 10- Don't Recognize Account

Credit Bureau Name

Credit Bureau Address

Credit Bureau City, State, and Zip

Date

Your Name

Your Address

Your City, State, Zip

Your Date of Birth

Your Social Security Number

Dear CREDIT BUREAU NAME,

Re: Account Name and Number

I am contacting you because I have found some information that is inaccurate on my credit report.

The date-of-last-activity you are reporting for this account don't match my records. I request that you verify the information and remove any inaccurate information from my credit report as quickly as possible. The items in question are:
CREEDITORS NAME AND ACCOUNT NUMBER

After doing so please provide me with an updated credit report reflecting the changes.

Thank you for your time,

YOUR SIGNATURE, YOUR FIRST AND LAST NAME

SAMPLE LETTER 11- INQUIRY REMOVAL

[Date]

President   *****SENT VIA CERTIFIED MAIL*****
Company
City, State, Zip

RE: UNAUTHORIZED CREDIT INQUIRY

Dear [President's name]

I recently discovered that your company ran an unauthorized report on me on [date]. I did not authorize such an inquiry and demand that you contact [name of credit reporting agency] immediately and have your inquiry deleted from my credit file. Pursuant Section 609 of the Fair Credit Reporting Act, You do not have a permissible purpose to pull my credit report hence invaded my right to privacy and may subject to a fine.

If you have any questions, please contact me at the address listed below.

Thank you for your prompt attention to this matter.

Sincerely,

YOUR NAME
Address
City, State, Zip

SAMPLE LETTER 12- UPDATE TO REQUEST COMPLETENESS OF ACCOUNT

[Date]

Credit Reporting Agency/Bureau
City, State, Zip

RE: REQUEST TO UPDATE FOR COMPLETENESS OF ACCOUNT HISTORY

To Whom It May Concern:

I received a copy of my credit report and am disputing information concerning my payment history. Accordingly, I am requesting that you investigate my dispute and add the attached history of payments to my credit file under the Fair Credit Reporting Act, § 611(a) [15 USC 1681i (a)].

I am requesting an updated copy of my credit report, which should be sent to the address listed below. According to the provisions of § 612 [15 USC § 1681j], there should be no charge for this report. Additionally, if you contact any entity (person or company) in order to make the necessary updates, please provide the names, business address and telephone numbers so that I may follow up directly if needed.

If you have any questions or need additional information, please contact me at the address listed below.

Thank you.

Sincerely,

YOUR NAME
Address
City, State, Zip
Social Security #

Letter # 13- Frivolous Letter Rejection

[Date]

Credit Reporting Agency/Bureau
City, State, Zip

RE: FRIVOLOUS LETTER REJECTION

To Whom It May Concern:

I am in receipt of your letter stating that my dispute of items in my credit report was "irrelevant and frivolous." I am upset that your credit reporting agency would try such a blatant stall tactic. I am demanding that you reinvestigate my credit file under the Fair Credit Reporting Act Section 611 [15 USC 1681I]. You have no way to ascertain the legitimacy of my action without investigating the items in question.

Enclosed is a copy of my original letter and credit report with the disputed items highlighted. Additional stall tactics on the part of your organization will be reported to the Federal Trade Commission.

If you have any questions, please contact me at the address listed below.

Thank you.

Sincerely,

YOUR NAME
Address
City, State, Zip
Social Security #

Chapter 8
Advanced Credit Disputing Techniques

Proficient credit repair is much more than just sending letters to the credit bureau. The credit bureau dispute process is based on the Fair Credit Reporting Act requirement that disputes be investigated.

Those disputes are highly effective to help remove inaccurate accounts off your credit reports. Sometimes, creditors are resistant, though, even when you know the item is inaccurate and should be deleted. And when this happens, it can be very frustrating.

This is where Advance Credit Repair Tactics come into play. These tactics are how you dispute and remove your most recent and harmful inaccurate accounts. And unlike credit bureau disputes, advanced disputes work within hundreds of laws, not just the Fair Credit Reporting Act.

These disputes are designed to challenge the creditor for compliance with numerous federal laws. Leverage is the main point of Advance Credit Repair Tactics. Your creditor is using the credit report as leverage to get paid. They are even willing to manipulate the data in their favor with the intent of worsening your credit.

If you don't feel you should have to pay an invalid debt, you might think you don't have a lot of leverage to fight back with. Actually, you have a lot of leverage to use to get your items deleted from your reports.

There are over 200 consumer laws that are designed to protect your rights as a consumer. Your creditors commonly ignore these laws. They blatantly break the law, counting on you not knowing your rights well enough to challenge them. And the truth is, you would have to be an attorney to know and understand all the rights you actually have.

I have put a few common advanced techniques and dispute debt validation letters in this chapter. You can also research online and find a few more advanced letters which might fit your individual needs. The tactics and few letters in this chapter will help you delete your most harmful accounts by challenging the creditor on compliance with some of these consumer laws.

Legally Creating a New Credit File

If you follow the instructions carefully in this section, it is completely legal and effective if you want to bypass the entire dispute process and have numerous derogatory items to remove from your report. Evaluate your scenario and decide if this method would be better for you.

You can create an entirely new credit file by legally changing your name. I discovered this method when my name changed when I got married and went through the proper channels of getting an updated social security card with my new name. Up until this point, I didn't know all the tactics of removing derogatory items and disputing methods, but I was determined to have my credit clear. By this time, I had effectively removed all derogatory items except a bankruptcy that continued to be reported. I had already removed the old address that was associated with the bankruptcy. So after my new personal name was updated with the bureaus and I sent another bankruptcy dispute letter it finally came off with no other push back from the credit bureaus. It had created what was considered a MIXED FILE. I was grateful and my score rose over 154 points. I had finally done it and entered into scores above 750+. Here are the steps to this tactic.

STEP 1: Go to your local courthouse with a name change petition and have it notarized for a new name and name change order. Keep in mind , you can change anything from your last name only, your 1st and last name, middle and last name, or your complete full name. However you should not have your new last name start with the first letter of your current last name. Remember the credit bureau system is a matching system.

STEP 2: Change your address. Remember it can not be an address you have ever used before. I discussed this in an earlier chapter of how to effectively obtain a new address from either a friend or relative or renting a PO Box that reports as an address from UPS or ipostal.com.

STEP 3: After you have new address, obtain a new SS card from the SS office by taking your name change order and ask for a new card. Your SSN will stay the same and this will not affect anything legally or your benefits.

STEP 4: Take your new name change order and get a new Drivers License from the DMV. This changes your identity and creates a new computer DMV record. This is also effective for those who need to establish a new drivers record and erase any previous DMV records. All vehichle registration data for any car that you have purchased or owned is stored by Experian data who owns AutoCheck.

STEP 5: Change your name of your current auto title and registration to complete the completely legal process for establishing a DMV auto record. This is particularly beneficial to those who seek a new clean driving record and lowered insurance rates. All past driving points or speeding tickets will no longer be counted against you.

STEP 6: Update your new name with your employer. You should also update your new name with vital records or health department in the state where you were born to obtain a new birth certificate reflecting your new name if you need to obtain a passport as well.

For all schools you have attended you will need to send a certified copy of your name change order to request they change your name for your school records and degrees earned.

STEP 7: Apply for a credit card on the Internet or locally, which will establish your new file with all three credit bureaus. You can also have someone add your new name as an authorized user on their account and apply for a few secured cards at your local bank. Do not contact a company with whom you have good credit and have the company put any good account under your new name. Do not report and credit you had before your name change as this will re-enter all the negative accounts also under both your old and new names since files will be crossed referenced. This will merge your new file with your old file and this entire process will have been in vain.

How Advanced Letters Work

The secret to advanced disputing is to challenge creditors on laws you believe they are probably violating. Many of the advanced dispute tactics involve requesting information from your creditors directly. This is documentation they have to supply to you by law.

For example, the Fair Billing Act requires the creditor supply you with many things upon your request. The required documents include all your billing statements, and detailed breakdowns of the debt allegedly owed, just to name a few.

In the dispute letter, the creditor is given the options of supplying the documentation, as required by law, or dispute the item from your credit report. Many advanced letters will also outline the repercussions the creditor will face if the item is not deleted.

These include official complaints being filed with the necessary state and federal entities. You also have the right to civil penalties, not to mention opening the door to a possible class action lawsuit.

The creditor faces all these repercussions for breaking the law and not storing the required documentation. And all will be forgiven if they simply delete the item from your report. This is just an example of how an advanced letter works. You find the creditor's violations, and then use those as leverage to get your invalid items removed from your credit report.

We stress permanently, because in this kind of disputing, the creditor is voluntarily removing the negative item. This means you stand little chance of having that item re-reported again on your report because they voluntarily deleted it.

Another example of an advanced dispute is challenging a collection company for HIPPA violations. Just by reporting a medical collection on the credit report, the creditor is violating medical privacy laws. The underlying principal of Advanced Dispute Tactics is the threat alone will get the item deleted from your credit report. Remember to only use these methods on accounts you know to be inaccurate.

The threat to sue, threat to file complaints with the Federal Trade Commission and Secretary of State, the threat to start a class action lawsuit against them, even the threat to investigate them further, is enough for most creditors to delete the item rather than deal with the headache.

Creditors prey on unknowing consumers. And out of 400 of those consumers, maybe one will actually ever challenge them on anything. In almost all cases, they would rather deal with the 399 consumers who have no idea what is going on and leave the other one educated person alone. This is especially true when you are catching them clearly violating the law and you outline your intentions to hit them in all the places that hurt the most.

NO company wants problems with the FTC and Secretary of State. NO company just ignores the threat of a lawsuit, especially when they know they are in the wrong. NO company waives off the threat of a nationwide class-action lawsuit against them.

It just doesn't make sense for them to fight back knowing that on one hand they face this, and on the other hand they simply delete a credit item they will probably never get paid to begin with from one person's credit report.

This is why advanced disputing works so well. The secret is to know and understand the laws enough to know what and how to challenge.

Mailing Advanced Letters

You can continue your credit bureau disputes for different reasons and work on some advanced methods, simultaneously. Find the best letter which fits what you want to verify with your creditor or addresses your specific dispute purpose.

Make sure you enter the account name and number on the dispute letter and don't forget to sign it. Then mail your letter to your creditor directly. All your creditors are listed on your credit report. You can obtain their addresses from the reports they return to you in the mail or through your credit monitoring service report.

These letters go directly to your creditors. Do not mail them to the credit bureaus or they will do you no good. Remember, the credit bureaus only dispute reasons. These disputes challenge and threaten, and you need these to land in your creditor's hands directly.

Make sure you mail your disputes to your creditors directly. Then keep an eye on your credit report for results. Many of these advanced letters require the creditor do certain things. But the law does NOT require that the creditor respond to your dispute.

The only way you will the result is on your report, your creditors will typically not respond to you by mail if they delete items based on your advanced letters. This is why it is essential you monitor your credit reports for the results of your advanced disputes.

I have included a few advanced dispute letters that you can use. You might need to do some further research online to find letters which better fit your unique situations or hire a professional credit specialist or attorney familiar with consumer credit law.

Goodwill Request

Creditor Name   Your Name

Creditor Address   Your Address

Creditor City, State, and Zip   Your City, State, Zip

                                  Your Date of Birth

                                  Your Social Security Number

Date

Dear CREDITOR NAME,

Re: Account Name and Number

I am writing this letter in order to request your help and understanding. Back in _____ when the negative item was listed], I lost my job and made a couple of late payments, even though I hated paying late. I do feel bad about it even now. However, I did get current on the account (listed above) as soon as my financial standing improved.

 I have in fact made timely payments since then. I've been working hard to make financially responsible decisions and get better control of my money.

I am now buying a home but having difficulty in receiving an affordable mortgage rate due to the negative listing on my credit report. Thereby, I would request you to kindly remove this negative item as a gesture of goodwill. Your kind gesture would be sincerely appreciated.

Thank you for your time,

YOUR SIGNATURE

YOUR FIRST AND LAST NAME

Debt Validation, Fair Billing Act and Fair Debt Collection Practices Act

Creditor Name *Your Name*
Creditor Address *Your Address*
Creditor City, State, and Zip *Your City, State, Zip*
  Your Date of Birth
Date *Your Social Security Number*

Dear CREDITOR NAME,
Re: Account Name and Number

This letter is being sent to you to inquire into the validity of a debt you are reporting on my credit report. Be advised that this is not a refusal to pay, but a notice sent pursuant to the Fair Debt Collection Practices Act, 15 USC 1692g Sec. 809 (b) that your claim is disputed and validation is requested.

This is NOT a request for "verification" or proof of my mailing address, but a request for VALIDATION made pursuant to the above named Title and Section. I respectfully request that your offices provide me with competent evidence that I have any legal obligation to pay you.

Please provide me with the following:

- What the money you say I owe is for;

- Explain and show me how you calculated what you say I owe;

- Provide me with copies of any papers that show I agreed to pay what you say I owe;

- Provide a verification or copy of any judgment if applicable;

- Identify the original creditor;

- Prove the Statute of Limitations has not expired on this account

- Show me that you are licensed to collect in my state

- Provide me with your license numbers and Registered Agent

At this time I will also inform you that if your offices have reported invalidated information to any of the 3 major Credit Bureau's (Equifax, Experian or Trans Union) this action might constitute <u>fraud</u> under both Federal and State Laws.

Due to this fact, if any negative mark is found on any of my credit reports by your company or the company that you represent I will not hesitate in bringing legal action against you for the following:

- Violation of the Fair Credit Reporting Act
- Violation of the Fair Debt Collection Practices Act
- Defamation of Character

If your offices are able to provide the proper documentation as requested in the following Declaration, I will require at least 30 days to investigate this information and during such time all collection activity must cease and desist.

Also during this validation period, if any action is taken which could be considered detrimental to any of my credit reports, I will consult with my legal counsel for suit. This includes any listing any information to a credit reporting repository that could be inaccurate or invalidated or verifying an account as accurate when in fact there is no provided proof that it is.

If your offices fail to respond to this validation request within 30 days from the date of your receipt, all references to this account must be deleted and completely removed from my credit file and a copy of such deletion request shall be sent to me immediately.

It would be advisable that you assure that your records are in order before I am forced to take legal action. This is an attempt to correct your records; any information obtained shall be used for that purpose.

Thank you for your time,

YOUR SIGNATURE. YOUR FIRST AND LAST NAME

Debt Validation, Fair Debt Collection Practices Act

Creditor Name　　　　　　　　Your Name
Creditor Address　　　　　　　Your Address
Creditor City, State, and Zip　　Your City, State, Zip
　　　　　　　　　　　　　　　　Your Date of Birth
Date　　　　　　　　　　　　　Your Social Security Number

Dear CREDITOR NAME,

Re: Account Name and Number

I am continually being called on the telephone by your firm over this alleged debt. I'm sure you are aware of the provisions in the Fair Debt Collection Practices Act (FDCPA), and I am requesting validation of this debt.

I am requesting proof that I am indeed the party you are asking to pay this debt, and there is some contractual obligation which is binding on me to pay this debt. I request that you stop contacting us on the telephone and restrict your contact with us to writing, and only when you can provide adequate validation of this alleged debt.

To refresh your memory on what constitutes legal validation, I am giving a list of the required documentation:

- Complete payment history, the requirement of which has been established via Spears v Brennan 745 N.E.2d 862; 2001 Ind. App. LEXIS 509 and
- Agreement that bears the signature of the alleged debtor wherein he agreed to pay the original creditor.
- Letter of sale or assignment from the original creditor to your company. (Agreement with your client that grants you the authority to collect on this alleged debt.) Coppola v. Arrow Financial Services, 302CV577, 2002 WL 32173704(D.Conn., Oct. 29, 2002) - Information relating to the purchase of a bad debt is not proprietary or burdensome. Debtor must phrase their request clearly to

> obtain: The source of a debt and the amount a bad debt buyer paid for plaintiff's debt, how amount sought was calculated, where in issue a list of reports to credit bureaus, and documents conferring authority on defendant to collect debt.
- Intimate knowledge of the creation of the debt by you, the collection agency.

I'm sure you know, under FDCPA Section 809 (b), you are not allowed to pursue collection activity until the debt is validated. You should be made aware that in TWYLA BOATLEY, Plaintiff, vs. DIEM CORPORATION, No. CIV 03-0762 UNITED STATES DISTRICT COURT FOR THE DISTRICT OF ARIZONA, 2004, the courts ruled that reporting a collection account indeed is considered collection activity.

While I prefer not to litigate, I will use the courts as needed to enforce my rights under the FDCPA.

I look forward to an uneventful resolution of this matter.

Thank you for your time,

YOUR SIGNATURE

YOUR FIRST AND LAST NAME

YOUR ACCOUNT NUMBER WITH THE CREDITOR

LAWSUIT NOTICE

DATE

BUREAU
ADDRESS
CITY STATE ZIP

Attn: Legal Department;

To whom it may concern;

I am writing to you to inform you that suit is being filed against BUREAU due to its refusal to correct the items outlined below. The items in question have been addressed with the creditors directly as well as BUREAU and they have complied it is BUREAU that has refused to correct the items in question and have received confirmation of this fact with each respective item except those that are deemed fraud. This willful wanton misconduct will no longer be tolerated. If the items outlined below are not corrected without exception upon receipt of this notice permanently as outlined then legal action will be taken within 14 days. You are already in violation of the FCRA without exception. If this notice is not complied with fully without exception or deviation legal action will be taken and no mercy will be shown.

Previously your office had assigned AGENT to aid in the clean-up following my repeated identity theft and things were cleaned up. However, you have taken her away and items have reappeared and now you will be held accountable for your actions or inactions as may be applicable. If legal action is required I will go back the entire statutory period and will take legal action for each and every violation that has occurred that you failed to comply with in the statutory period. This will then make you additionally responsible for actual damages, treble damages, court cost's, legal fees as well as statutory fines for your well documented will full noncompliance with the ACTS. Each violation will be dealt with.

The creditors in question that are not deemed frauds have submitted updates to you but you have failed to implement them as I have copies of these and the creditors have submitted these corrections to the other bureaus and they have fully complied it is only BUREAU that has failed to comply. I have outlined the items below and the required action for each and deviation will not be tolerated.

1. ITEM 1
2. ITEM 2
3. ITEM 3

You have previously been given the required 30 day period required by law and you are now in violation. If legal action is required every and all courses of action will be pursued. This is the last opportunity that will be given you to resolve this matter amicably. All responses are to be in writing no electronic format no exception.

Respectfully,

NAME

Chapter 9
Dealing with Identity theft

Identity theft is when a consumer's personal information is used by someone else for personal gain. This crime is quickly becoming one of the biggest and most costly crimes in America. In 2008 alone, over ten million people were victims of identity theft.

Identity theft happens in many ways. Some common forms of ID theft are credit card and utilities fraud, bank and loan fraud, and even government fraud. Identity theft destroys credit profiles, so prevention is always the best solution.

Prevention means flagging your own reports, making it harder for anyone to gain access to your credit profile, and keeping an eye on your credit report monthly with a good credit monitoring service. Or you can consider hiring an outside company to monitor your credit for you.

Safeguarding your personal information is also very important to ID theft prevention. Shred all personal documents instead of throwing them away. Change your passwords regularly on your personal accounts also.

Be very protective of your identity and monitor your credit profile regularly to prevent identity theft. But if all else fails, your identity is stolen, and your credit report is damaged, the rest of this chapter will show you exactly how to deal with fixing the damage.

Fixing Damage with the Credit Bureaus

Identity Theft cases are handled differently than any other dispute. This is due to FACTA having a certain section dedicated to how these disputes MUST be handled.

The credit bureaus have very strict restrictions on how they handle identity theft cases. If you take the steps listed below, by law they must delete the negative item from your report within 4 days. There is no grey area in FACTA. If you are a victim of legitimate ID theft you will want to file a police report and follow up with an FTC affidavit form to have the items removed with the credit bureaus.

This is an extremely effective way to have these items permanently removed from your credit report, guaranteed. After you have filed your police report you can pick up your report when the officer has it completed. Make sure you get a copy of the police report, as it will be required to file the official Identity theft report with the credit bureaus.

Identify Theft Federal Trade Commission Complaint

The second main component of an official Identity theft dispute is a fraud complaint with the Federal Trade Commission. After you file your police report, go online to file your official ID Theft complaint with the FTC. To get started visit https://www.ftccomplaintassistant.gov/.

This "complaint assist" system with the Federal Trade Commission will then walk you through the complaint process. Answer the questions as you make it through the complaint process. These are the basic questions they ask to get the dispute started. The rest of the questions are then specific to the identity theft instances that occurred.

And at the end, of course, they then ask for all your personal information and allow you to then print the entire form. You will then need to use this form along with your police report to file your official Identity theft complaint with the credit bureaus.

Filing the Complaint with the Credit Bureaus

Now you should have your police report and complaint form from the Federal Trade Commission. You will want to include those with this identity theft dispute letter.

Date
Your name
Your address
City, State and zip

Credit agency name
Credit agency address
City, State and zip

Re: (*your social security number*)

Dear (*Insert Credit Agency Name*),

I am contacting you regarding some fraudulent accounts appearing in my credit file.

I have recently become a victim of identity theft. I am providing you with copies of the necessary documents (*enclose copies of police report and fraud complaint*) to verify the fraud allegations. The accounts in question are: (*list the Debt Collector or Collection Agency along with the account numbers*)

Unfortunately these are not my accounts. Please remove these items from my credit report.

Sincerely,

YOUR SIGNATURE, (*Print your name*)

Ensure that you complete the dispute form with the creditor's name and account numbers. Also, ensure you include your police report and FTC complaint form. You can then mail off your dispute and await the response.

To learn more about Identity Theft and how the Federal Trade Commission handles these cases visit http://www.ftc.gov/bcp/edu/pubs/consumer/idtheft/idt04.shtm.

Fraud Alerts

A fraud alert will be placed on your report when you have an identity theft case or when you request that one be added to your report.

You have most definitely seen ID theft protection companies on TV. What these companies do is solicit the credit bureaus to have a "fraud alert" placed on your credit report. This fraud alert makes it tougher for people to access your credit report and use it to apply for new credit.

The alert is placed on the report and the creditors that you then apply for see this alert. They will then require additional identifying documentation from you to process your application. So if you put a fraud alert on your report, then go to apply for a car loan, the car dealer would then require additional ID from you to verify your identity.

Fraud alerts do give you an extra layer of protection against ID theft, as the creditor must follow strict guidelines in verifying your identity. But keep in mind; you will be the one who is most hassled by a fraud alert on your report.

Each time you need to apply for new credit, you will be put through an extra series of steps to verify your ID. This will slow down your approval process, for sure, and in some cases, this can become a bit of an annoyance.

So only put a fraud alert on your report if you know someone is trying to steal your identity and use it in applying for new credit. Fraud alerts can easily be placed on your credit report by you. There is no need to pay a company monthly to do this for you, as the process is fast and easy to do this yourself.

Identity Theft companies do also charge you to monitor your report for suspicious actively. You can monitor this yourself, there is no need to have a company do this for you as this is a free request with the bureaus.

Even if you do hire another company to monitor this, you still need to access your credit reports 1-2 times per year on your own to verify that no unauthorized activity is happening to your reports. You know what is on your credit reports better than anyone else. So your eyes need to see your reports to insure your ID is safe and your credit is in-tact.

Placing a Fraud Alert on your Report

Filing a fraud alert on your credit is fast and easy to do. You can either call the credit bureaus or file for your alert online. Below are the phone numbers and web addresses which you will need to file your complaint.

The fraud alert will instantly be placed on your report, whether you are requesting the alert through phone or on the bureaus' websites. A statement will be added to your credit reports stating that you may be a victim of fraud and that creditors should take additional steps to protect your identity before extending credit.

Here is the contact information you will need for the bureaus to file for this fraud alert.

Equifax Fraud Department   (888) 766-0008

Web: https://www.alerts.equifax.com/AutoFraud_Online/jsp/fraudAlert.jsp

Experian Fraud Department   (888) EXPERIAN (888-397-3742)

Web: www.experian.com/fraud

Trans Union Fraud Department   (800) 680-7289
Web: www.transunion.com/corporate/personal/fraudIdentityTheft/fraudPrevention/fraudAlert.page

When you request your alert online, the web page will ask for some basic information on who you are. The form is pretty simple and easy to complete. When you call in to request your alert, you will be asked similar questions.

Once you complete the questions a red flag will show on your report for this new fraud alert. Any future creditor you then apply with will see this alert and request additional identification to issue credit.

Fraud alerts are a great way to prevent identity theft. They add another layer of protection to ensure your credit profile is protected. And these alerts are fast and easy to have placed on your credit reports.

Chapter 10
How to Use Pay for Deletion Method

Earlier in this book, you learned how paying off a collection can actually hurt your credit scores. The reason is that you update the date-of-last-activity on your report. This then keeps that account on your credit report longer and the bureaus read the pay-off as recent negative activity which adversely affects your credit scores.

There is only ONE way to fix credit--remove the negative items from the report. Paying them to $0 balances won't help. Instead, you need to remove all evidence of the item's existence, as if it never happened.

The credit bureaus don't have a memory. This means your report is a snapshot of what your credit is in a certain point of time.

If you get a negative item deleted from your report, future creditors will NEVER know it was ever there to begin with. And your credit scores will react to the deletion the same way. They increase as if the negative account was never there.

To fix credit, you MUST have the item deleted. This is why I advise clients to never pay off their negative items without trying to dispute and investigate first.

Through the dispute process, you will remove most of your negative accounts from your reports. The items you can't get removed through deletion, you might want to negotiate to have them removed.

Your <u>leverage</u> is the balance you still owe on the debt and the fact that the creditor or collection company wants to still get paid. This is the leverage you will need to use that the item is DELETED from your credit report.

You DON'T want to have the creditor tell you they will UPDATE your account or report it as a $0 balance. You must be CLEAR that you want the item DELETED from your report, and that is the only way you will pay off that debt.

This process is called **Pay-to-Delete** for obvious reasons. You are PAYING to have the item DELETED from your report.

Understanding the Collection Process

Most of your debts will be negotiated by a collection company. And in many of these cases, these collection companies purchased the debt from Wall Street. In some cases, a creditor will hire a collection company to pursue you. But after two years in most cases, and one year in many cases, the creditor "writes-off" the debt on their side.

They then sell the debt in a bad debt pool on Wall Street for literally 5-25 cents on the dollar. Then a collection company purchases this debt in "bundles." A bundle is really an Excel file with a bunch of consumer data.

It might contain 10,000 consumers who have defaulted with that creditor. The list might have the name of the consumer, address, phone number, and account details. In many cases with collection companies, this is ALL the evidence they have to try to collect on that debt. This is why disputing removes so many collections, especially with advanced tactics.

In reality, very few collection companies even have what they are required by law to have in order to collect on the debt in the first place. Once challenged, they concede and delete the item knowing they don't have the documentation they need.

Now you understand who you are talking to when you speak with collection companies. And also know they will almost always accept at most 50% of the debt. This is because they bought the debt for 5 cents on the dollar.

So if your credit card balance was $1,000, the collection company purchased the rights to that debt for $50. Yes, they will gladly accept a payoff of $500.

The only case where they won't is when they successfully file a judgment, which is rare. They are tough to negotiate with when a judge has determined that you have to pay them. Again, this is rare, and in most cases they will gladly negotiate with you.

When to Use Pay-to-Delete

There are a few times you want to consider paying off a debt to have it deleted from your report. The first instance is where you have tried all other dispute methods, unsuccessfully. This might occur if you have disputed to the credit bureaus many times and used many advanced tactics that have also not worked to have the item deleted.

If you have used the dispute methods in this book, you should only have a very small percentage of creditors who need paid off to delete the item. In those few cases the debts are probably pretty recent and the creditor or collection company might have all the records and documentation they need to report the debt. So they will keep fighting back because they think they have enough evidence to validate the debt.

Another case where you might want to use Pay-to-Delete is when the debt keeps being reported by new collection companies. These debt pools are not just sold to one collection company.

Many companies purchase this debt, then try to collect. Later you will find out how to use this to your advantage for a Pay-to-Delete. This buying of your debt is not the main issue. The problem occurs when multiple companies start reporting the debts against you, one after the other.

So let's say you had a bad Capital One debt. You disputed it and were successful and the item was deleted. Two months later, your credit score goes down and you see that a new collection company is now reporting that debt.

So you turn around and successfully dispute and delete that account. Another month passes and again another company is reporting that debt. In this kind of case, you might want to consider a Pay-to-Delete. This might especially be true if you need your credit scores to be at a certain number to qualify for financing.

When the debt keeps getting sold, then reported by different companies, your scores will continue to drop each time the new collection appears. You might choose just to negotiate and get that debt paid off so no more companies buy and re-report the debt. Or, you might just continue the disputing and delete the collections as they appear.

The choice is yours, in that instance, but a Pay-to-Delete would permanently remedy your problem. These are the most common cases where you might want to consider a Pay-to-Delete.

How to Get an Item Deleted By Pay-to-Delete

To get an item deleted you want to first find out how much you want to pay on the debt. The common end place is 50% settlement, but that doesn't mean you can't negotiate more.

First, figure out what you are willing to pay on the debt, then call the collection company. You will usually have someone assigned to your account, so write down the name of that person. Let them know that you are serious about paying off that debt, but don't have all the money to pay it all off. Still, you want to "do the right thing and put it behind you."

This is the language they will try to speak at you with, so hit them with it first so they take a step back. Ask them what they can accept for payoff, and listen to what they offer. From here a negotiation begins between what they are offering you and what you want to pay.

If you are willing to settle for 50%, the negotiation will in most cases be very short. This is because they usually accept those terms with no issue. Once you get numbers worked out, and have agreed to a price, then you will want to let your representative know that you need to insure the item is **DELETED** from your credit report.

And let them know you need something in writing stating the item will be deleted from your report. This is where they might begin a play on words. They might tell you they will update or change the account. Don't accept anything other than them agreeing to DELETE the item.

Insure that they confirm themselves that they will DELETE the item from your report and that they will give it to you in writing. If they won't give it to you in writing, record the phone call. One way or another, get confirmation from them and try to do it in writing.

If They Say Yes

You are all set. Get your letter from the creditor or collection agency agreeing they will delete the item from your report, and pay them what you agreed on.

You will then want to send a copy of this letter to the credit bureau with a general dispute letter, stating the account is inaccurate and demand deletion. Wait for the results from the credit bureau and keep an eye on your credit monitoring account. Ensure that this item does get deleted.

If the creditor gives you the letter and agrees, you should then see that the item is deleted. I have never seen a case where this doesn't happen. But make sure you get the letter agreeing that they will DELETE the account from your credit reports. Then you should see the item removed 40-45 days later.

If They Say No

In most cases, creditors and collection companies will not just roll over and give you this letter. They will typically put up some type of resistance. You already know the first tactic they will use, telling you they will UPDATE your report. And you also know to insist on a deletion, not an update.

They will also tell you that they CAN'T delete the item from your report. They will tell you it is against the law, they don't have the authority, or any number of other excuses. The truth is they have every right to request the item deleted. Further, the process for them to request this is VERY simple.

They only complete a simple form known as a Universal Data Form. This is basically the same form the credit bureaus use to process your credit disputes to your creditors. The process takes less than five minutes for them to complete the form and send it back to the bureaus. And it is 100% legal and they 100% have every right to do this.

Even though they will sometimes insist they can't delete the item, no matter what they say, KNOW that they absolutely can delete that item. If the collection company tells you they CAN'T delete the item, request clarification. Tell them, you CAN do this, you just won't do this.

Then ask that before you move forward with the conversation that they acknowledge that this is something they CAN do. This will rattle them, but be insistent that they acknowledge that they CAN do this. You might even want to say to them, "all you need to do is complete and return the Universal Data Form."

That statement shows them that you know what you are talking about. Then be very nice and tell your representative that you KNOW it can be done. Let them know you also understand that they might not have the authority to authorize that. Let them know again that you are ready to pay off the debt as agreed, you just need confirmation the item will be deleted.

Then politely tell your representative that if they don't have the authority to authorize this, that you would like to speak with a supervisor who does have that authority. Talk this out with your representative or get a supervisor on the phone. In most cases you will be dealing with collection companies.

You can let them know that you are serious about paying off the debt. If they are serious about taking your money, then they will agree to take five minutes to complete the universal data form and everyone wins.

Remind them that you already have the original creditor on your credit and there is no reason for their account to also be reported. You want to do the right thing and pay off the debt; they should do the right thing and delete their duplicate report.

Also, remind them that if they won't do this, then they are not serious about taking your money. You will just wait to speak with another collection company for that debt that will take your money and delete the item.

They might tell you that the item would remain on the report in that instance and remind them that they are saying it will remain on your report even if you pay them anyways. In the end, demand confirmation they delete the item in return for payment.

If they won't accept this, DON'T pay it off. You will gain nothing and lose the only leverage you have. Try to work this out with the collection company. If they won't work with you, keep disputing.

Another collection company will report who you can deal with. Then when this company no longer holds the debt, POUND them with disputes. They won't waste tons of time fighting back when they don't hold the debt, and have nothing to gain by fighting with you.

Don't pay that debt off without them agreeing to delete. And don't accept their excuses if they tell you they can't do it. Stand your ground, so they know you are serious and know what they can do. In most cases they will agree to delete in return for payment, if you are insistent.

Chapter 11
Legal Liability and Statute of Limitations

Credit repair will NOT remove your legal liability to your debts. Even if you do delete your negative credit items from your credit report, you will still legally owe that debt. If you pay off the debt or collection, the damage will still remain to the credit report.

The DEBT OWED and CREDIT REPORTED are two completely separate elements. If you still owe a creditor money, then you delete the account from your credit report, you still owe that creditor money. They can still legally pursue you for that debt, if they so chose to do so.

If you have a judgment, or garnishment of wages, having the item deleted will not make that debt go away. You will still owe the debt, even if the item is not on the credit report. The purpose of repairing your credit is so that future creditors who review your reports will not see the prior damage.

This will help you get approved for the financing you need, and at a very good interest rate. You will also be able to re-negotiate with your current debtors when your credit profile is repaired, lowering those interest rates and payments.

There are endless benefits to having a great credit profile. Just keep in mind when you see those reports coming back with all those deletions, you do still legally owe those debts. You might require the services of an attorney if you want to pursue the creditor, in the case to remove this liability.

Statute of Limitations (SoL)

Almost all the creditors on your credit report have a statue of limitations for how long they can attempt to collect on a debt. The statute of limitations is the legal time frame that the debt can be pursued through the court system.

There are some accounts that have no statute of limitations. Below is a list of most of those debt types.

- Federal Student Loans
- Most Types of Fines
- Past Due Child Support
- Taxes and Tax Liens

The statute of limitations is typically based on the state you live in now or the state the debt originally occurred in/ the state you were in when you originally applied for the debt. Every state is different, so you might want to research the limitations in your state on your account types. You can research for your state's civil debt collection codes.

According to the Fair Debt Collection Practices Act, most UNSECURED debt expires in 3-6 years. Contracts such as car loans expire after six years. Judgments can last up to 20 years and can indefinitely be renewed.

Those dates are typically based on the date of default (when you stopped making payments), but some contracts might extend to the original contract date. This also varies based on state law.

These statutes are important to you for a few reasons. Firstly, it there are some disputes based on the debtor not being able to collect on the debt due to the statue of limitations expiring.

Secondly, this is why you never want to make any kind of payment to a collection company. The time they can collect would then extend from the time you made your last payment to them. This is why some collection companies make it so easy for you to pay with payments.

But even the Federal Trade Commission warns, "WARNING! While the statute of limitations (SoL) is running or even after it's expired, making ANY payment or signing a promissory note can reset or restart (depends on your state law) the statute of limitations."

Finally, you don't want to push your disputes too far with creditors who can still pursue you in court. If you start attacking an original creditor with a year old debt, your disputes might just prompt them to excel your case to the courts. This is rare, but it does happen.

The older a credit item is, the more successful your disputes will be. This is partially because the creditor has less documentation, and in large part, due to many older accounts being outside of the statute of limitations.

The creditor doesn't really gain anything on responding to all those disputes, as they know they can't collect on the debt legally, anyways. The opposite is also true. If a creditor knows that you owe them money, they have current documentation clearly supporting their case, they might pursue you in court.

If you start attacking them with credit disputes, you will increase the probability that some of those might come after you. Don't get really scared off by this, just know it can happen. And try to limit your attacks to creditors where you know the debt is truly invalid.

Credit Reporting Statue of Limitations

There are really two types of statutes of limitations. The first is the time frame in which the creditor can collect on the debt. You just learned all about this type of statute of limitations. But the second type of limitation applies to how long the creditor can actually report the debt to the credit bureaus.

Most credit items can only be reported for seven years on the credit report. Some public records, such as judgments, can remain for ten years. Tax liens can be reported indefinitely, based on certain requirements.

These are the common limitations for how long creditors can report the debts on your credit profile. But don't forget to evaluate your state laws to see how long you can legally be pursued for those debts.

How Collection Companies Manipulate SOL

Collection companies want you to believe that by paying the debt you are helping your credit. But unless they delete the item from the report, you are actually hurting your credit. This is due to the "date of last default." That date reflects the date you last made a payment on the account. So if you stopped paying CHASE in November 2013, the date of default on your credit report will reflect as 11/2013.

This means that account should drop off 11/2020. That is, seven years past the date you last made a payment on the account or date of last activity. In the same example, let's say you settled the account with collections 11/2015. You thought you were doing a good thing. You settled it for pennies on the dollar and the creditor agreed to update your report.

In reality they update a $0 balance and then update the date-of-last-activity to the date you paid off the account. After all, the day you pay collections now becomes the last day you made a payment on the account. Now, since you paid it off 11/2015 and that is the new date-of-last-activity, that account will now stay on your report until 11/2022, which is seven years past the date you last made a payment.

If left alone, the account would have naturally dropped off 11/2020, seven years past your original default date. Now it will remain until 11/2022 because, when you paid off the collection, you established a new date-of-last-activity. Sure, the balance is reported as $0. But this won't help your credit scores at all.

Your credit score is literally a mathematical model which reflects your risk of going 90 days late on an account within the next two years. If you let an account go into collections, you are obviously a much higher risk to go 90 days late in the future. But if you pay off that account after it is in collections, you really are no lower risk of going late again.

To try to elaborate, your risk is that you let the account go bad to begin with. Your risk isn't lower if you pay it off after it goes into collections. Truly, you are still the same risk of defaulting in the future, even if you did pay it off after the fact.

This is exactly why Fair Isaac doesn't give you credit in your scores for paying off collections. You are not a lower risk if you let the account go bad, no matter what you do with the account after that point. Paying off collection accounts do not help your credit scores in any scenario.

PRIVACY OPT-OUTS

After you have cleaned your credit file, it would be advantageous if you had your private and personal information opted out of public forums and domains. You want to do all you can to preserve your newly established good personal credit and operate more privately. I have included opt outs to remove your info from said lists.

PRE-APPROVED CREDIT LISTS

888-5OPTOUT (888-567-8688)
Removes your name from creditor pre-approval lists sold by the 3 main credit bureaus- Equifax, Experian, TransUnion

EMAIL LIST REMOVALS

Email: www.e-mps.org
Professional association of elected state general attorney. The site provides links to each state's website, where you can find consumer protection information that is state specific.
Federal Trade Commission (FTC)
CRC 240 Washington, DC 20580
www.ftc.gov
877-382-4357

TELEPHONE LISTS REMOVAL

Website: https://www.donotcall.gov/
Email: www.the-dma.org
Mail: Direct Marketing Association
Telephone Preference Service
P.O. Box 1559
Carmel, NY 10512

DIRECT MAILING LIST REMOVAL

Website: https://www.directmail.com/mail_preference/
https://www.ims-dm.com/cgi/optoutemps.php
Mail: Direct Marketing Association
Mail Preference Service
P.O. Box 643
Carmel, NY 10512

Chapter 12
Building Business Credit Profiles and Scores

Business credit scores and profiles are completely different than consumer credit scores. One of the biggest differences is that business credit scores and profiles reflect a business's credit risk, while consumer credit scores evaluate an individual's risk. Business credit scores depict a business's risk of going 90 days late on any of their financial obligations in the next 12 months.

Most business credit scores range from 0-100 with 100 reflecting the best score that can be obtained. Business credit scores are based on only one single factor: whether a business makes prompt payments to its suppliers and creditors within the agreed upon terms of payment.

For example, prompt payments will produce a credit score of 80. A 70 score reflects paying 15 days behind, 60 score is 22 days behind, a 30 score reflects paying 90 days behind, and a 20 reflects paying bills 120 days late.

One of the main benefits of business credit scores is that a business owner can easily obtain an excellent business credit score quickly, within 30-60 days. All that is required to obtain a business credit score is accounts being reported to the appropriate business credit reporting agencies. Once paid-as-agreed accounts report on the business credit report, the business owner is rewarded with an excellent business credit score.

Business credit profiles and scores are crucial to helping business owners obtain credit with no personal liability. Many business owners use their personal credit for their business. This creates a problem, as those business owners become personally liable for their business debts.

Business credit allows business owners to build credit for their business without a personal guarantee. This means the credit that is being used for the business has no personal liability from the business owner. So in case of default, the creditor cannot pursue the business owner or the owner's personal assets, such as bank accounts and homes.

As positive business credit scores and profiles are established the business owner will not need a personal guaranteed to be approved. Since there is no personal guarantee required with many business credit sources, there is also no personal credit check required. This means business owners can still be approved for business credit even if they have challenged personal credit.

Even business owners with excellent personal credit should obtain business credit. By having both a personal and business credit profile, business owners see there purchasing power double. Plus it is a great idea for business owners to use business credit so they can avoid the personal liability that comes with using their personal credit for business purposes.

Business credit scores are important, as they determine how much credit a supplier will issue to a business owner, the interest rates that will be paid, how much money will be lent, and even what type of insurance premiums will be paid

There are three major reporting agencies for business, Dunn and Bradstreet, Experian, and Equifax. Each have their own unique database of business owners and their own score models.

Dun and Bradstreet

Dun and Bradstreet, commonly known as D&B, is a publicly traded company with a headquarters in Short Hills, New Jersey. D&B provides information on businesses and corporations for use in credit decisions. Currently, they hold over 200 million company records on file.

D&B's roots track back all the way to 1841, with the formation of the Mercantile Agency in New York. In 1933 the Mercantile Agency joined with R.G. Dun & Company and became known as Dun and Bradstreet.

Dun & Bradstreet offer many products and services to consumers and businesses. Some of these include risk management products, such as the Business Information Report, Comprehensive Report, and the DNBi platform. These provide current and historical business information, primarily used for lenders and financial institutions to assist in making credit decisions.

D&B also offers sales and marketing products, such as the DUNS Market Identifier database, Optimizer, and D&B Professional Contacts, which provide sales and marketing professionals with business data for both prospecting and CRM activity.

Just as Equifax, Experian, and Trans Union are leaders in the consumer credit reporting arenas, Dun and Bradstreet is the leader in business credit data.

The main credit score used in the business world is known as a Paydex score, provided by Dunn and Bradstreet. This number assesses a business' lending risk much the same as a consumer credit score reflects a consumer's individual credit risk. D&B describes this as the unique dollar-weighted numerical indicator of how a firm paid its bills over the past year, based on trade experiences reported to D&B by various vendors.

The Paydex Score ranges from 0-100, with 100 being the highest score you can obtain. Having a Paydex business score of 80 or higher is very good, as scores below 70 are very bad.

Experian

Experian is the largest supplier of information worldwide. They provide information services in 65 countries across the globe. Experian is listed on the London Stock Exchange (EXPN) and is a constituent of the FTSE 100 Index.

Experian's main purpose is to report financial information and performance across North America, UK and Ireland, Latin America, and Asia Pacific. They are recently providing credit bureau access and solutions in Morocco, Saudi Arabia, Kuwait, India, Pakistan, Iran, Singapore, and even Turkey.

Experian's commercial database, BizSource^{SM}, provides information on U.S. companies and extensive data on the small businesses. Experian Business provides credit risk evaluation services to businesses based on their own business owner independent databases.

Experian, one of the three major consumer credit rating bureaus, is now providing business credit evaluations for over 27,000,000 small businesses and corporations to detect early signs of trouble by monitoring key customers, suppliers, & partners. Experian's model is designed for companies that provide goods and services to small business.

Some of the items listed on Experian's reports include...

- Business credit scores and credit summary
- Key facts about the business
- Corporate registration and contact information
- Summaries of collections and payments
- Uniform Commercial Code filing information
- Banking, insurance and leasing information
- Bankruptcy filings
- Judgment filings
- Tax lien filings

Experian's business credit score has over 800 variables which are calculated into a score known as Intelliscore. Credit scores range from 0-100, with a lower score indicating a higher risk for serious delinquency.

Experian does provide both consumer and business credit risk models and sometimes they provide blended reports with data from both consumer and business reports. Experian and their Intelliscore are commonly the second choice for lenders behind the Dunn and Bradstreet Paydex score.

Equifax Small Business

Equifax has been in business over 100 years and has its headquarters in Atlanta, Georgia. They employ over 7,000 people across 15 countries, including Europe and Latin America. Equifax does trade on the New York Stock Exchange under the symbol EFX and is a member of Standard & Poor's (S&P) 500® Index.

Equifax, one of the three major consumer credit rating bureaus, is now providing business credit evaluations for over 22,000,000 small businesses and corporations to detect early signs of trouble by monitoring key customers, suppliers, & partners.

Equifax offers a business scoring credit model knows as Equifax Small Business Enterprise/ Equifax Small Business Credit Risk Score. Equifax's Credit Risk Score model is designed for companies that provide goods and services to small businesses.

This model integrates credit or trade history, business demographics, and financial payment history into its score calculation. The score was created to enhance risk assessment throughout the account life cycle by predicting the probability of a new or existing small business customer becoming seriously delinquent on supplier accounts, or bankrupt, within a twelve month period.

Credit scores range from 101-992, with a lower score indicating a higher risk for serious delinquency. For example 0-9 is low risk, 10-20 is average risk, 21-30 is above average risk, 31-40 is high risk, 41-69 is the highest risk, and 70 indicates the business has filed for bankruptcy.

Equifax also offers a PayQuo score, which is similar to most other business credit scores. This score can be obtained alongside a business credit report.

With PayQuo, a 90 or higher indicates early payment, 80 means the debt was paid 10 days or less past the due date, 70 means it was paid 20 days past the due date, 60 score indicates payment 30 days late, 50 scores indicate the debt was paid 60 days late, 40 scores mean the debt was paid 90 days late, 30 scores reflect payment was made 120 days late, and 20 scores indicated payment was made over 120 days late.

There are also four reason codes which indicate top factors that impact the credit score for a better understanding of risk. Equifax even includes a business failure score which predicts the risk of a business filing for bankruptcy. Equifax does provide both consumer and business credit risk models, but there are considerable differences between the two.

It is essential for business owners to build their business credit profiles and scores so they can limit their personal liability. By having both personal and business credit profiles, business owners double their borrowing power and look more respectable in the business community. These are only a few reasons every business owner should become familiar with their business credit scores and then leverage those scores to greatly increase their borrowing potential.

Conclusion

Your credit is your financial life and this impacts a very BIG part of your personal life. With a positive credit profile, you can leverage your credit to live a different type of life and grow your financial dreams. You will get approved for the new credit you want, own your dream home, purchase a car with a very low interest rate and payment, get approved for high limit credit cards, and receive approvals for 0% credit cards.

You will have the available credit lines you need in case of emergencies and record low interest rates and payments on all your credit items. This will give you the money to save for your retirement, even your childrens education. Most importantly, good credit will stop you from living paycheck-to-paycheck and give you the extra money you need each month to live the life of your financial dreams.

Completing this book now means you are a credit expert. You now know the secrets behind your credit scores, and how to control your own scores. You know how the credit system works and understand the history behind the credit bureaus. You now even know how to dispute inaccurate items thorough credit bureau and advanced credit disputes to have those items deleted.

It is my intent to have provided you with the knowledge and tools you need to obtain and maintain an excellent credit profile. Put your knowledge to use today and get started on correcting your credit file. Once your profile is positive, make sure you use all the tips in this book to keep your credit profile positive and high as possible. Great credit can be leveraged to propel you to increase gains financially and step into bigger and better financial opportunities in life.

Remember to keep your mind focused on the positive vision that you have for your life and nothing will be impossible to those that believe and maintain the right mindset and speak words according to their vision.

About the Author

Bianca and her team have helped educate many consumers and business entrepreneurs across the country in repairing their credit and starting new businesses. Her passion to help others achieve financial freedom actually grew from seeking remedy to fund her own businesses and learning how to master key building blocks of personal and business credit. Bianca is the CEO and founder of Savvy Credit Associates, an author, online entrepreneur and credit consultant.

For contact inquiries or more information , visit her at www.savvycreditboss.com

www.ingramcontent.com/pod-product-compliance
Lightning Source LLC
Chambersburg PA
CBHW031631210526
45464CB00004B/1844